THE WISDOM OF THE IRISH DRUIDS

By Michael McGrath,

Archdruid of Tara and Ireland.

Beyond the Triple Spiral
On the fair side of the Sun,
A dragon roars in a cave
Under a world that's just begun.

COVER: The Mound of the Druids, ever since St. Canice's cathedral and round tower, Kilkenny city - photo by Michael McGrath, professional photographer, Kilkenny City 0877560725.

Cover attribution:
The Wisdom of the Irish Druids
by Michael McGrath,
Archdruid of Tara and Ireland.
Cover and editorial design by vvbdesign

The Wisdom of the Irish Druids

Copyright © 2023 Michael McGrath

All rights reserved. No part of this publication may be reproduced, distributed, or transmitted in any form or by any means, including photocopying, recording, or other electronic or mechanical methods, without the prior written permission of the publisher, except in the case of brief quotations embodied in critical reviews and certain other noncommercial uses permitted by copyright law. For permission requests, write to the publisher, addressed "Attention: Permissions Coordinator," at the address below.

Published by Druid Press.

Email: photographerofkilkenny@gmail.com

FRONT COVER PHOTOGRAPH , "The Mound of the Druids" by Michael McGrath, professional photographer, Kilkenny city, Ireland R95 E1WA, mobile (353) 0877560725, PhotographerOfKilkenny@gmail.com

Preface

CHAMPIONS OF THE SOVEREIGNTY OF THE LAND.

After I completed this book a lady druid advised me of the need for some preliminary words suited to people who have only begun the consideration of druidry. Other geniuses have made suggestions to me about how to make the book more palatable to use.
Thus I suggest that one first browses through the book as a whole, though preferably not in the bookshop. Then read it in the order it appeals to you. Top of the list of answers to enquiries I have received through the years: "Druidry is not a church, so it is best to remain in your present church- if you have one. Druidry can only enhance your spirituality in your present religion."

Druids opposed the building of the M3 motorway through the Tara Valley. And we proved right to do so as up-to-date reports show that not as many drivers use that motorway as was claimed they would.

Many prefer to take the old toll free road that seems just as good today. It was a mindless destruction that is now proven. I wish, as Archdruid, to convey this good news to all the activists who fought to save Tara.

We see ourselves as champions of sovereignty in its noblest sense, of the Land, the sacred sites and of our national heritage. Legislation that attacks our heritage, such as the ancient Irish freedom to cut turf in the bog, is not seen as coming from the people, but from usurpers carrying out EU dictates who are abusing their power.

We are now ready to march against the Hate Act, that they are imposing to enslave the Irish people this very week, to reclaim our constitutional right to unfettered Freedom of Expression under Article 40.6.1 of our Constitution.

French druid and author Michel Raoult has written of Ireland as "home of the druids par excellence." We are needed more than ever out on the land as activists , and in the cities preserving our old buildings, to be champions of the living environment.

We also need to be prepared to stand up against State tyranny to come, such as new laws to jail people for keeping certain literature on their computers and bookshelves.

We must continue to stand in where the MSM media has sold out and protect decent citizens from being wrongfully criminalised and jailed for what are now being pursued as Thought crimes. How brilliant a prophet Orwell was , but even he would be staggered to come back today and witness the deadly progress of the monolithic State tyranny that grinds the Irish down like no country in the world outside of North Korea.

State tyranny, we thought, was over - but it's now returning in more subtle, more dangerous forms, such as prosecuting citizens for thought crime. Seven hundred years ago they burned a young 24 year old woman, Petronilla Di Media, at the stake in the centre of Kilkenny on 3rd November on suspicion of having the wrong thoughts and being "in league with the devil".

She was just an innocent young girl. We must always be wary, especially those of us regarded as outliers, and therefore vulnerable, of those in power.

They destroyed many of the sacred sites along the Tara valley - and then Ireland collapsed, bankrupt morally and economically to its knees in 2008. . Whoever in power thought the Ancient Ones would stand idly by and let it go unpunished has had to think twice about it ever since!

Michael McGrath,
Archdruid.
Kilkenny, May Day 2023.

TABLE OF CONTENTS

Introduction..11
Chapter One: The Fiery Conversion of Ireland..........................13
Chapter Two: The Twilight of the Druids..................................19
Chapter Three: The Rebirth of Druidry.....................................29
Chapter Four: Some Ancient Irish Druids.................................31
Chapter Five: The Mound of the Guardian................................39
Chapter Six: The Lost Wisdom of the Druids...........................47
Chapter Seven: Druidcraft..59
Chapter Eight: The Psychic Fires of Ireland.............................67
Chapter Nine: The Theory and Practice of Druidry..................71
Chapter Ten: Manipulating the Force.......................................85
Chapter Eleven: Spellcraft - the Ritual of Cursing...................91
Chapter Twelve: The Nature of the Druids.............................101
Chapter Thirteen: Shaman, Druid and King...........................107
Chapter Fourteen: Druid Divination..117
Chapter Fifteen: Revelation. A Druid reflects on Tarot..........125
Chapter Sixteen: Druidic Crystal Scrying 131
Chapter Seventeen: The Celtic Tree Oracle...........................143
Chapter Eighteen: In our own rite...151
Chapter Nineteen: The Graceful Druid....................................159
Chapter Twenty: The Truth against the World.......................165
Chapter Twenty One: The Atlantis Archipelago.....................175
Chapter Twenty Two: Chief Druid of His Time.......................181
Resources..195
Epilogue...213
About the Author...221

Introduction

ENCOUNTER OF A DRUID KIND.....

Whisked along a tunnel of light, he hovered in front of the old oak door, a small low studded brown door. The keystone above the door is a huge rock crystal inscribed with the druidic symbol of the triple spiral. Dazzled by kaleidoscopic whorls of otherworld colours from the crystal, he reached out to grasp the bronze door knob. Effortlessly the door opened. Inside, in the centre of a cavernous room a golden treasure chest lay open amid rivulets of wine red blood flowing across the black stone floor. The surface of the chest formed a flashing blue screen. A head began to form on it, a familiar face - he had seen it through many lifetimes, the face with no eyes. ~ It was Mog, properly called Mog Ruith. pronounced Mogree. Now he felt at home and at ease as the tall longhaired and bearded figure loomed up in front of him. He reached out to greet the Bornless One, but Mog stopped him in his tracks with a wave of his dragon- headed staff.

"Careful, Archdruid, touch me and you may not go back into the world you have come from, where you are reeded.
"Of course", the Archdruid agreed, stepping back.

"Archdruid, I know you are writing a book of ours for the world. I have a weakness for the shape, the feel, the smell, the very touch of a new book. He tapped the golden chest with his staff, Ancient parchments sailed up out of it and floated towards the Archdruid who grabbed them eagerly.
"The world thirsts for our secrets, use these clues and riddles well, Archdruid, such wisdom has the blood of druids upon it!" The Archdruid found himself lying across a grassy wet mound of Tara as he woke. As he moved to get up, three large parchments fell from the folds of his robes. As he picked them up he complained loudly to himself; "Typical of Mog, he expects me to make a book out of these flimsy sheets, the old miser "

Something clipped him across the back of the head. Startled, he glanced up. There it was, a black raven winging up into the clear air. Mog was at it again! Some passing American tourists pointed their cameras in his direction, giving him wary looks as they fired away. The Archdruid, a fearsome apparition seldom seen amongst Christians, waved at them. Worried, they backed away. He wondered why. They must be mad, he reassured himself. He gathered up the parchments, slid down the grassy knoll, and headed out the gateway. For Druid headquarters back in the Liberties of Dublin. That afternoon he was dictating the book to Dunphy, the best ghostwriting journalist in Ireland, in the rear lounge of Mulligan's pub. This book would tell secrets to the world, Dunphy declared, as the Archdruid ordered another round of Guinness.

Chapter One

The Fiery Conversion of Ireland

"The great kings of the pagans wail ever in burning. The hosts of Jesus without a fall, they are joyous after triumph .. the faith has grown, it will abide until the Day of Judgement; guilty pagans are carried off, their forts are not inhabited ...

The oldest cities of the pagans concerning which proscriptive right has been affected, they are empty without worship, like Lugaid's site (Tara). Paganism has been ruined, although it was illustrious and widespread."

This is a contemporary description from an old Irish manuscript from about 800 AD. Note the grim satisfaction of the monkish chronicler at the burnings - the Final Solution to the Druidic problem. For an earlier genocide had just happened in Ireland of Irish druidic society. From thereon the druids would survive under the guise of Fili and Faidh. The triumphalist chronicler goes on to contrast the now desolate sites of Tara, Cruachu, Aileann and Earmhain with the bustling Christian monasteries of Armagh and Kildare.

It's easy to see that the attitude of early Irish clerics to druidism was unenthusiastic. Equally noteworthy is the consistent condemnation of contemporary Druidism that is still evident in our present time.

The great festival of Samhain was held at the time when Earth crossed the powerful Encke stream with meteoric activity at its height. We have only to read the chronicles of Gildas, the Roman priest, to see how Christianity would have impressed itself on the fifth century Irish, propagandized against their own druids who were helpless in the face of the great catastrophe. Gildas describes disastrous thunderbolts striking the British Isles - calamities used by Patrick and the incoming missionaries who promised worse to come as signs of the wrath of God, if they did not convert. Clube and Napier in their book "The Cosmic Winter" quote Gildas who wrote his chronicles two hundred years after that fifth century terror:
"The fire of righteous vengeance (which) wasted town and country ... horrible it was to see the foundation stones of towers and high walls thrown down bottom upwards in the squares, mixing with holy altars and fragments of human bodies." As Britain and Ireland were subjected to dramat-

ic deforestation, which could have been caused by massive forest fires in the middle of the fifth century when Patrick arrived, he would have made great play of this failure by the Druids - the very custodians of the forests - to save the people against the anger of the Christian god."

The "Confessions of Patrick" describes how he wandered for miles and miles across a desolate Ireland, a wasteland of burnt forests, vast wilderness where there was no human, animal or plant life to be found. The populations of Britain and Ireland were so devastated that many of the survivors moved across the sea to Brittany for safety.

The success of the conversion was assured as the missionaries exhorted those returning to stay on, promising that the new Christian god would protect them from all harm.

Towards the end of this era of mass conversion, the kings deserted Tara. Indeed, that ancient site has every appearance of being hit by a meteorite. The scale of these disasters of meteorites showering down upon these islands, devastating the lands and forests, reached a height of frenzy in the ninth year of the mission of Patrick in 441 AD and was far more terrible than any similar occurrence in any other part of the world since the Middle East had been hit three thousand years previously.

There has been nothing like it since. Not only were the forests destroyed but the climate was affected as well, with comet and meteorite dust acting like a sun shield as deep freeze conditions spread across the land.

Observers from as far apart as Spain and China reported seeing an unusual comet in 441 AD, accounting for the catastrophe as described by Gildas. And during this time the Earth passed directly through the dust trail associated with Encke's Comet and the Taurid meteors too. It was immediately after these terrible events that the missionaries moved into all parts of Ireland on direct orders from Rome.

They may have been part of an international relief team at the time but they certainly took advantage of the total collapse in the Irish social establishment with the old druid order destroyed, unable to offer any resistance . Colliding asteroids can change belief and whole religions too.
Not only the unlearned peasantry but many of the Irish intellectuals of the time, particularly the bards well versed in the Greek classics, were readily taken in. The missionaries themselves fully believed that they were living

in a time of the wrath of God.

The Roman clerics employed such arrant propaganda mercilessly, as they were specifically trained to. The druids had no chance - as astronomers, they knew the truth. But in 441 AD the people of these islands had seen the heavenly terror with their own eyes. The survivors passed 'the wrath of God' down to their children and their children's children. Crashing meteorites moved faith, triumphed over fact, and ensured a bright start for the new church in the ancient homeland of the druids.

Throughout its history the earth has been subject to sudden catastrophes that give rise to new beliefs among people in desperation, such as you have today with school children panicking over carbon related climate change, as they are misled by mass media and their own teachers. In "The Reversing Earth" physicist Peter Warlow puts forward a unifying explanation of these events - including the ice ages, the frozen mammoths, the biblical floods, the dinosaur extinction, reversals of the earth's magnetic field, sudden changes in culture, climate - and religion!

WORLDS IN COLLISION.

Our way of life must not be disturbed. Wo/man occupies a friendly planet in its comfortably stable part of a safe solar system, generously provided by a loving god. All around us there is chaos, collapse and catastrophe. We see on TV at least, if not through astronomers' telescopes, entire galaxies explode, huge collisions out in space. But our own galaxy, the Milky Way, is naturally a quiet corner of the universe, a secure place to be. The land trembled but that was long ago. In the present, here and now, there is peace and calm on and around our planet home, remote in space and time, separate from the violence of elsewhere in the universe. Many school children are upset over what they are wrongfully told is climate change caused by proliferation of carbon dioxide. Druids have always known better. The cairns, stone circles, dolmens and standing stones across the land are an open book. They quietly speak a language of their own to those of us who have taken long years to understand. They had certain energy networking to do across the land along the ley lines that we dowse. Getting back to modern science, that all these panicking schoolkids deserve to learn instead of the alarmist bunkum they're filled with - even by their own teachers - druids always concentrated upon the Sun when it came to the weather. It's the mainspring of all our weather on Earth. So is Carbon Dioxide, necessary for plant life and our own survival on the planet. It's only when carbon is mistreated in manufacture that it becomes toxic - but

even then it does not change the climate.
Several investigators have claimed that the rotation rate of the Earth upon its axis actually changes at times of severe atmospheric storms from solar outbursts. Livshits, Sidorenkov and Starkova of the Russian Institute for Terrestrial Magnetism claimed that there is a definite relationship between the earth's rotation rate and the magnetic field of the Sun. And it is the rate of sunspot activity on the surface of the Sun that principally causes the Earth's climate change - principally, I say, because there are lunar and planetary influences in the calculations too.

EVEN THE STONES SPEAK…

There were serious disturbances in our solar system within the last ten million years. Velikovsky, to his credit, thumbed his nose at the lies and slander cast at him by some of his fellow scientists in stating that there were marked disturbances of our solar system only a few thousand years ago. Right across Ireland, Britain and parts of Europe, thousands of cairns, stone circles, dolmens and standing stones quietly speak a language of their own to those of us who have worked for long years to read that great 'book of the land'. We know that all these structures had energy building and networking to do across the land. Newgrange, Stonehenge, Avebury, Callanish, Carnac - these are just some of the bigger more famous structures that we will be talking about. Most of the circles are not exactly circular. They are egg-shaped. Professor Thom also discovered that they were built to a common unit of length. People who knew the value of Pi and the relationship of the sides of a right angled triangle built Newgrange. They also knew the golden mean ratio and crystal properties.

They knew all this thousands of years ago in Ireland. The druids ran the first university type facilities throughout Europe. Professor Thom concluded that some of these sites were astronomical observatories - and as we shall see so were the round towers of Ireland that served a multiple purpose. The original purpose of these ancient sites was for astronomy as employed for calendrical purposes. These megaliths were not built by astronomer-priests. Forget the priests - they were astronomers!
Peter Warlow writes in "The Reversing Earth":

"They had a need to make accurate and comprehensive astronomical Measurements. The planets were doing something for which they were aptly named. They were wandering." A wandering planet - wandering not in today's stately fashion - is not a very nice thing to have in the solar system. In the same vein the main purpose of the round towers of Ireland can be queried. Everybody wanted to know if and when they were about to be affected in the way that their ancestors had been, the ancestors from whom they had inherited their knowledge.

THE CIRCLE IS COMPLETED

Excavations carried out of the sites where the ancient astronomers of Stonehenge lived indicate that they were an unusual and elite group, whose food supplies were brought in reverence from elsewhere by others who were hunters and gatherers serving this elite. It seems that they received provisions as a form of tribute from the awestruck people living roundabout.

It would be nice to think that, having built Newgrange in Ireland, some of these Atlantean druids moved on to build Stonehenge in Britain and Carnac in Brittany along their route across Ireland, Britain, ancient Gaul and ancient Greece to finally build the Temple of Karnak and the Pyramids of Egypt. It is implicit in the mathematics and the astronomical alignments of all these ancient constructions. They gave rise to such awe among the native Egyptian that they were worshipped as gods and goddesses.

In time Moses was initiated into the secrets of the High Priesthood of Egypt and together with Aaron brought the sacred knowledge into the land of Israel.

There it flourished among the initiates, the scribes of the Old Testament and among the Essene of Qumran on the shores of the Dead Sea. There, in the wilderness of Judea, came a time two millennia ago when a young man came ·among them to study and train for 18 years, to undergo many initiations and to acquire the expertise of utilising the secret knowledge.

Twelve hundred years later during the crusades, the Military Order of the Temple, the Knights Templars discovered the ancient wisdom and brought it back with them to Europe. Rome became horrified at the prospect of those secrets becoming known - that could spell the end of the Church, it was feared. The Templars were suppressed, arrested on the orders of the Pope and the chiefs of the Order executed. Those Templars who escaped arrest fled to the relative safety of England, then to Scotland and Ireland. From the public burning at the stake of Jacques de Molay, Supreme Commander of the Order of the Temple in Paris on Good Friday 1307, seven hundred years ago, it was 200 years on to the Reformation. The adepts in turn brought about the Renaissance, the Enlightenment and the French Revolution that drove the Church from France for a while. A druidry that had never fully died out was manifesting itself across the centuries. Events had turned full circle.

They are spiraling now...

Chapter Two

The Twilight of the Druids

When the Church encouraged the Emperor Constantine's image of himself as a messiah, appending the title 'The Great' to his name, it commenced the establishment of itself as the religious arm of the State.

That State was the Roman Empire then ruling nearly all the known world by the sword. The Church could now embark upon a gigantic mission of conversion and, with the help of that sword, dictate religion unto all nations. There followed the period of decline and fall of indigenous religions and the final killing-off of Druidry throughout Britain and Gaul.

Constantine, the new messiah, would achieve for the builders of the new Church what the original messiah, Jesus, had failed to do three hundred years earlier. Constantine is indeed great. He is the great founder of the Roman Church. Moreover, on the strength of a document which is supposed to have come to light in the eighth century, the so-called 'Donation of Constantine', he was held to have conferred some of his own Imperial power on the Papacy. And it was on the basis of this document that the Church abrogated to itself the right to create kings and princes, as well as to establish its own authority in the world.

By virtue of this document the English Pope Adrian IV granted Ireland to the Norman King Henry 11, naming him 'Prince of Ireland' even before the Norman Conquest of Ireland commenced in 1169 AD. Finally, Constantine presided over the Council of Nicaea in 325 AD which set up the Roman Church.
The aims and objectives of the Church were set and its beliefs and dogmas brought into force after a hurried vote confirming Christ's divinity. The Nicene Creed, said by all Catholics at mass to this very day, was composed. From there on any deviation was to be regarded as heresy and punishable as such, often by execution. Seeing things in this light, we can appreciate the terrible plight the European Druids faced back in the fourth century. We know the hollowness of the usual apologia for the disappearance of the Druids, that they readily 'converted'. We can guess the horrific nature of that conversion, if it ever took place. Evidence is slowly emerging today of a holocaust of the Druids throughout North West Europe in the fourth century, when only the Druids of Ireland and Scotland survived

outside the Roman State. The 'Donation of Constantine' itself turned out to be one of the greatest confidence tricks in the history of the world. On such sands of time is built the edifice of the Church in the world. We shall leave it there as we turn to sources, ancient and modern, and let them tell us all about the Druids.

THE NEW STATE RELIGION

Being acquainted with the New Testament, I am mostly in agreement with its moral precepts. But the druids and many ancient religions preached such high morality and practiced miraculous things upon the Earth long before the Church of Constantine in 325 AD.

It was made the compulsory religion of the empire by his successor, the Emperor Theodosius seventy years later. Shortly before the collapse of the Roman Empire, a momentous decision was made to control men's minds by the new religion. The druids, those valiant leaders of Celtic national resistance, who urged on the fight for freedom from under the Roman Yoke, ended up crucified along the Appian Way.
Now only the Gaels of Ireland and Scotland, unconquered in the field of battle, remained to be converted. Already in the year 314 AD, long before Patrick, the Irish Church was sufficiently well organised to be able to send bishops to the Synod of Arles. The Irish Church was also represented at the Council of Arminium in 359 AD.

Caesarius of Arles, who died in 453 AD, indicated that the old Gaulish belief in the gods and goddesses of springs and woods was still very much alive. Christian and Druid lived side by side. Both congregations even prayed and worshipped together at certain sites, such as the Oak Church of Brigid in Kildare. There was little acrimony between Druid and Christian, rather an intermingling of belief.

Missionaries came in through Cork, Ardmore and Lismore on the southern Irish coast, directly across the sea from Spain around 200 AD. There were others too. Remnants of Roman settlements have also been found from this period at Stoneyford, eight miles south of Kilkenny City and in north County Dublin. They are thought to be traders from the Roman Empire. Naturally, those who were Christianised Romans would have brought their beliefs along with their merchandise.

The Arkites hold that Jesus was brought by his uncle, Joseph of Arimathea, to Cornwall when he was on a trading mission there to buy tin. This was circa 27 AD when they are supposed to have visited Glastonbury - and by extension, Tara. So convinced was the Arkite English landlord who owned Tara that the Holy Grail was buried there that he brought hundreds of workmen in to dig up the ancient hill. They dug for the Ark of the Covenant too, but were stopped by a campaign to save Tara, led by W. B. Yeats, AE and Douglas Hyde at the end of the Nineteenth century. Luckily for posterity there were no JCB machines then, or like Tailteann there would be precious little of our sacred hill left today.

Patrick, who came to Ireland in 432 AD, is credited with the work of several missionaries. A man called Patrick did in fact arrive to convert the Irish, but much of the work was done before he arrived. One of the characteristics of Patrick's religion was his belief in dreams. This is typically druidic. He regarded dreams as messages from God. He was the first to challenge the druids, that is, to introduce the element of 'Churchianity', of church competition, into Ireland. Until his coming everybody lived in harmony in their own spirituality. The Irish druids were neither organised nor ready for such an onslaught by a proselytising church. In fact they had never come across any church or religion which insisted on 'converting' people.

The druids were also powerless because they were the original innocents who could not recognise propaganda or come to terms with falsehood of any kind. They did not believe that the end justified the means. They did not believe that two wrongs make a right. Ireland was a land of innocence. Patrick preceded Augustine with his practice of re-consecrating and re-using the sacred Druidic places. Wisely he knew that whatever the religion preached the Irish would still keep on attending their customary places of worship.

Patrick's mission started fifty years after the Emperor Theodosius had declared Christianity to be the compulsory religion of his empire. The christianisation of Ireland was ongoing for two hundred years before Patrick ever set foot on the island. This is where history gets mixed up with myth.

The Culdees, the Celi De, the servants of God, had already established the Celtic Christian Church in Ireland before the arrival of Patrick. Seventy years before Patrick, St. Kieran of Saighir, patron saint of the Diocese of Ossory to this day, built his little church in Kilkenny, of all places on the site of what was to become in medieval times the Inn of the Witch, Dame Alice Kyteler, which today thrives in the heart of the Marble City as Kyteler's Inn.

Interestingly, Dame Alice had a familiar called Art, and a learned article in The Cauldron magazine traced Art back to druidic times when he was a deity. We have the great druidic King Cormac Mac Art (Cormac, Son of Art) for example. We wonder too - did the word Art really originate from the Latin word Ars, or has it in fact a history much further back in ancient Ireland?

Patrick was here by his own personal decision as he knew the Irish, druids and all, from the time of his captivity in Ireland, and therefore he wanted a peaceful conversion of Ireland. But he was also here on the orders of a Rome that did not concern itself overmuch with the means, to deliver the fatal coup de gras to the last surviving Druid Order on Earth and so put an end to Druidry forever. He was also sent to reorganize the Church in Ireland, which until then was little more than a druidic movement that recognized Jesus as the Son of God. Patrick did not, as legend has it, escape High King Laoighaire's soldiers on his way to Tara. He was travelling directly to Tara at the head of his large entourage that included troops, for what we call today a summit meeting of the heads of Church and State. This had already been arranged at the highest levels and with all diplomatic protocol.

At Tara Patrick sat with the High King and his Archdruid and far-reaching agreement resulted in the foundation of the Irish Celtic Christian Church, which was to persist in its own wayward style, despite the Council of Whitby, for over seven hundred years down to the Norman
Invasion. But the attitude of the early Irish clerics to druidry was unenthusiastic to say the least. Equally noteworthy is the consistent condemnation of contemporary Druidry at the time as a diabolical practice, as we see in the sources.

For instance the triumphalist author of Felire Oengusso around 800 AD notes with grim satisfaction:

"The great kings of the pagans wail ever in burning: the hosts of Jesus without a fall, they are joyous after triumph. The Faith has grown, it will abide until the Day of Judgement: guilty pagans are carried off, their forts are not inhabited.

"The old cities of the pagans(sen-chathraig na ngente), concerning which proscriptive right has been effected, are empty without worship, like Lugaid 's site. The small monastic sites have been occupied in twos and threes, they are monastic Romes (ruama) with assemblies, with hundreds, with thousands. Paganism (ingentlecht) has been ruined, although it was illustrious and widespread. The kingdom of God the Father has filled heaven, earth and sea.

A YOUNG DRUID

Even the hierarchy of the Roman Catholic Church in Ireland today tries to discourage overmuch devotion to the fabled Patrick. And for good reason too. Their problem is that he actually existed and he was running a much different church.

Patrick, from Bath it seems, was taken hostage by the all-powerful and much-feared raiders of the patriotic High King of Ireland, 'Niall of the Nine Hostages'. Niall had all that he wanted. The prevailing opinion among Irish Christians that he was simply a raider and a plunderer is such a pity. A true Irish hero, his attacking warships were the scourge of the coasts of Britain and Gaul as he sailed to the aid of his fellow Celts. Of course Niall deprived the Romans of some of their ill-gotten gains. Yes, he took hostages to ensure the proper treatment by the Romans of his fellow Celts - poetic justice, as hostage taking was a Roman custom! Our great warrior king has suffered fifteen centuries of vitriol - because his forces took a youngster called Patrick hostage.

As a young hostage Patrick was in fact privileged, as he was fostered out under ancient Irish custom to the Druid Miliuc. Of course, like everybody else, he had to work for a living, in his case as a shepherd on Slieve Mish. But he also sat and ate at the druid's table as his foster son and spent many an hour learning Druidic lore. Miliuc appears to have been a minor Druid. Patrick was as reckless as any of the young Celtic warriors that he had as friends around him, indulging in wine, women, song, dance, sport and hunting. In his Confessions there is mention of a 'wicked sin' he 'committed' at the age of fifteen. It would not have been of a sexual nature, as that was commonplace, accepted universally back then, and not regarded as a sin by either druid or Christian priest.

There is not a jig of evidence that it was of a homosexual or bestial nature. How 'hung-up' have Christians since become about sexual affairs - there was little attention paid to such in these early times. As Patrick was a young person of integrity, no less than the son of a deacon, it is doubtful if the 'sin' was just plain robbery, cattle rustling or downright stealing.

The only thing that could be regarded as a serious 'sin' in Roman eyes would be a druidic initiation. Had he actually trained to be a druid? Some druids accepted Jesus. Is this why his ecclesiastical superiors, although they prepared him for his mission to Ireland, refused to ordain him as a bishop ? Did they regard him as 'tainted'? At any rate when he returned to Ireland it appears that the druids were no match for him. Obviously he knew their ways. Was he one of them, and if so, how long did he remain a druid? And he had the advantage of the magical tale of the resurrection Jesus to tell, in an age when there was no TV or radio, and scant books either for the multitude. The native Irish chieftains and kings took to it like ducks to water..

It is quite clear that Patrick, not by any means the first missionary saint of Ireland, went much further than Augustine was later to do in adapting to druidry. He seems typically Celtic (from Celtic west Britain). He had blue-painted eyelids and hair shaved across his head in the druidic, not Roman, tonsure. He travelled like a chieftain, with an army of followers, craftsmen, bards, musicians, and soldiers too. Knowing all about the high standard of life and learning in the druidic colleges, he proceeded to the takeover of the ancient sites. Conversion of the native Irish of North East Ireland, where he preached, was an easy task. After all both cults taught survival after death and both believed in an in-dwelling supreme spirit. Druidry is always able to absorb more gods like Jesus, while as regards the Trinity, druids could hardly have asked for a more delightful rendition of their own belief!

So the Druidic training colleges were taken over and made into monasteries and nunneries. The word 'Druid' became strictly forbidden. The 'Patrick Mission' did not impinge on the self-isolation of the ascetic Culdees.

THE CELTIC CHURCH OF IRELAND

It was Christians of the Nazarene tradition, descended from Jesus through his brother James, Gnostic ascetics from the Egyptian desert, who came in on the shores of Southern Ireland around the year 200 AD. They were the descendants of some of the very first Christians from the Egyptian desert, who travelled along the north coast of Africa, beyond the remit of Rome, and came up through Spain to found their Diocese of Santiago de Compostela in Celtic Galicia. Now, with the advent of Patrick and the decline of the druids the Celtic Church came into its own in fifth century Ireland .

It was no longer consigned to the unofficial existence of non-recognition it had endured for three centuries. Centered in Ireland with 'provinces' in Southern England, Wales, Northumbria and Cornwall, it now made its grand entrance onto the ecclesiastical stage. Scotland and the Isle of Man were to join in the sixth century.

The missionaries who came into Ireland in the fifth century were unremarkable men. Yet, within a century, Ireland became the true centre of learning for the whole of Europe.

The wisdom, the philosophy and the science of the druid, coupled with the gnostic theology of the native Celtic Church, engendered a marvelous transformation in scholarship. Ireland shone as the centre of culture and civilisation. Scholars flooded in and with them vast quantities of manuscripts for safe-keeping and copying. The former druidic colleges, now famous monasteries, attracted students from all over the world.

Members of the various noble and royal families flocked to Ireland for their education.

The Celtic Church and Rome were so different in so many other crucial matters that something fundamental was involved. John McNeill in The Celtic Churches states: The issue between Romans and Celts went far deeper than the recorded exchange of arguments indicates, and he concludes: The ultimate issue was that of Celtic ecclesiastical autonomy against integration within the Roman ecclesiastical system. This separation was what the Irish druids had demanded! A closer examination of the Celtic Church reveals a much greater deviation from Rome than is generally acknowledged or even known. The Celtic Church had its own ordination rites for priests and these differed from Rome's. It had its own mass and liturgy, both of which incorporated non-Roman elements. It even had its own translation of the Bible - one that Rome deemed unacceptable. In flagrant denial of the Nicene Creed the Celtic Church consistently glossed over belief in the Trinity. And clerics of the Celtic Church seem to have followed in the footsteps of Patrick in ignoring the Virgin Birth.

As late as 754 AD, nearly a century after the Synod of Whitby was supposed to have patched things up, there were complaints to the Pope that Irish missionaries in Europe ignored the canons of the Church, rejected the writings of the fathers and despised the authority of the synods. The favourite saying of the Celtic monks, on the other hand, was The Celtic

Church brings love where Rome only brings law.

In 664 AD the Celtic and Roman Churches finally made peace at the Council of Whitby in Yorkshire.

But Rome would not have full control until the Normans came and imposed it by force of arms. In its time the Celtic Church drew upon a variety of texts independently of Rome.

In one curious instance a prayer is found from The Book of Cerne. Many texts are unique to Ireland. They are named, were used, but have never been seen. Some have been preserved and exist today in some archive, library or monastery in Ireland, a treasure trove comparable to the Nag Hammadi Gospels and the Dead Sea Scrolls.

Here the Celtic priest entreats most fervently ...

I entreat Thee by water and the cruel air. I entreat Thee by fire. I entreat Thee by earth. I entreat Thee by land and sea unresting ...I entreat Thee by the triad, wind, sun and moon. I entreat Thee by the compass of the tuneful firmament; I entreat by every stately-branching order, the host of the bright stars. I entreat Thee by every living creature that ever tasted death and life. I entreat Thee by every inanimate creature because of thy fair beauteous mystery. I entreat Thee by time with its clear divisions. I entreat Thee by darkness. I entreat Thee by the light. I entreat all the elements in heaven and earth. That the eternal sweetness may be granted to my soul ...Mo Drui Mac De! (trans: My Druid, Son of God).

The Hidden Tradition

Chapter Three

The Rebirth of Druidry

"Gloinne in ar gcroi, Neart in ar lamh, Beart do reir ar mbriathair." "Cleanliness in our hearts, strength in our hands, and our word according to our vows"

- The Triad of Honour given by the druids to Fionn MacCumhal and the Fianna.

Magicians and philosophers, priests and scientists, the druids were the guardians of the secret knowledge.
Skilled architects of the cairn- temples, they gained their wisdom from thousands of years of observation of the sun, moon, planets and stars. They were the counsellors of kings and gave judgment in the courts.
They remain with us today, not only in legend, but in the form of the modern initiatory societies who are actively exploring and restoring ancient lore as they attune to the faint voices of our ancestral druids across a void of fifteen centuries. The druid once again illuminates the western world with the great fire of vision presenting a wisdom once thought to be lost back there in the days of oral tradition. One thinks of trees and plants, esteemed by the druids for their healing powers, only now being re-discovered by modern medicine for their wondrous properties. One example, known as St. John's Wort, was recently stolen from the Irish people by legislation for control by big pharma.

Now proving to be powerful again, the rituals of natural magic were cast as superstition and the ancient Druidic lore of time and place usurped and thus rendered impotent. Throughout Britain and Gaul, druidry was attacked with particular brutality and force by the Roman Empire.

Later in Ireland the name Druid was outlawed, and all we held dear as sacred sites transformed by the Holy Roman Empire to its own benefit, enhancing its credibility off the backs of the vanquished druids. Across the land the druid returns, rekindling the golden flame, retracing the old straight tracks, a proud figure pointing to the sacred occult lore. For truly he saw it in the heavens and wrote it upon the Earth. And as he goes, as of old, he preaches a new environment of the spirit in a land laid waste, a land profaned, the beautiful blue planet he cries for, Goddess of his time.

The druid looks on, impassive, at flocks drowning in the Lake Isle of Innisfree. The Churchman may whisper frantically; "Do not let that Druid upon his royal and ancient hill or he may speak of seven centuries after Patrick when the Gael were heathen still, 'saved ' only by a certain papal bull of Adrian IV and the invading Norman army of Rome, of Strongbow slaughtering men, women and children in the streets of Waterford.

That druid may even tell that the waters of far-off Lourdes reported miracles two thousand years ago when it was the Shrine of Belisama - anagram for Masabiel - who was an ancient goddess of the druids of Gaul.

Today we dabble with the moon and the vernal equinox to fix the date of Easter - how very druidic. The followers of Odin celebrated it as Eostre, with the druid's egg thrown in for good measure. And for Thousands of years Newgrange has measured Christmas. The ancient druids were never inclined to share out the secrets with the uninitiated, but we have travelled a long hard road since then.

What we druids are doing is we are getting back to our Gaelic spirituality because the vision has gone so terribly wrong for so many in Ireland. We seek clarity. Faith may move mountains but only the clarity of our vision will move them to the right places. Seeing things in a new light we can appreciate the terrible peril of extermination our very own ancestors faced back in the fifth century and we know the hollowness too of the usual apologia for the 'disappearance' of the druids, i.e. that they readily 'converted '! We can guess at the horrific nature of that 'conversion'. Evidence to the contrary is slowly emerging today, that a persecution of druids occurred in the fifth and sixth centuries and culminated in genocide in the eight century AD. Finally isolated as the only druidic nation in the world, Ireland's golden age was brought to an end in relative peace as the newcomers negotiated with our kings and chieftains, and the illustrious Order of Druids silently disbanded. Ever since, we have been dotted in our ones and twos around the fringes of the Gaelic world.

Did a marvellous civilization wind its way in through the Milky Way as imaged in the triple spirals on the walls of Newgrange, or maybe there really was an Atlantis out there on islands off the west coast of Ireland? Fleeing the Flood they came our way and built Newgrange and Stonehenge and then went on to build the Parthenon of Greece and the Pyramids of Egypt. travelling on to eventually settle as Essenes at Qumran, where they taught a Shining One during his 'lost' eighteen years.

Chapter Four

Some Ancient Irish Druids

"And you, O Druids, now that the clash of battle is still, once more have you returned to your ceremonies and rites. To you alone is known the truth about the gods, or else unknown. The innermost groves of forests are your abodes. And it is you who tell us that the spirit has a body elsewhere, and that death, if what you sing is true, is but a midpoint in the longer life "
             - translated from Lucan in the reign of Nero (54 - 68 AD).

OLD JOHN McGRATH

The mizzling sky darkens over thatch collapsed by famine with black smoke belching from burnt barks of trees as the Romish year of Black '45 straggles the Emerald Isle. The old Druid had wandered the byways all his life, a seanchaidh telling and re-telling the ancient lore as it had come down to him through the ages from father to son, from the golden age when his ancestors were Archdruids of Munster, reigning as far as the eye could see from atop the Rock of Cashel. He sang in his native tongue in the sean-nos style of the fili. He played the old button accordion that he had won from a sailor at poker. He plied his craft and taught Irish dancing - jigs, reels and hornpipes - to the scions of the wealthy, of the Ascendancy, in the big houses throughout the province.

He was paid for his services. As the best music and dancing teacher in the south of Ireland the landlords competed for his art, especially the neighbouring De La Poer as they had a bit of a conscience. Their ancestors had taken most of the lands of his clan.

Left to him were a hundred acres that he never used. The neighbours traditionally grew their vegetables and raised their animals there. It was all a Druid had left to give them. The horror of the great famine was now striking as the potatoes went black in the ground. He survived with his art and guided his family through the pestilence that now stalked the land of Ireland, no county being devastated more than his own Waterford.

Now he lay dying in his old farmhouse. He had something on his mind. He had one right remaining, under tradition and ancient law still surviving, for his body to be cremated in the burning pit, as it was known, on the De La

Poer estate across the mountain. The skulls and bones of all the male line stretching back through time were piled up there, forming The Mound of the Bones, Cnoc na Chnaimh. He derived much of his power and inspiration from that sacred mound and wanted to add the experiences of his own lifetime to all the existences immanent there.

Through the weeks he knew he was dying his wife and family assured him he would be placed on top of that mound of his forefathers. But they had become devout Roman Catholics. Already they had the parish priest call to administer the sacraments to him, which he politely declined. His mind began to work overtime.....

He suspected that his wife and family and the parish priest were all in league to administer the sacraments to him the moment he fell into the sleep of death and bury him in the local Catholic churchyard in the parish of Rath 0 gCormaic. They meant well. They just didn't know.....

His wife's people, those Murrays, had the name of being altar climbers. He didn't trust them. One fine summer's day with the sun high in the sky, he rose from his deathbed when there was nobody around ...

That evening the alarm went up, and the clamour went out when they discovered he was missing.
The following morning they found his body, lying on top of his ancestral mound of bones in his traditional Druidic robes.

The dying man, well into his 'nineties, had risen, put on his best Druidic robes, saved for high occasions, and struggled ten miles across the mountain, the ensuing inquest concluded, to his ancestral mound.

But it was strange. Everyone was puzzled. He was known by all. Yet nobody had seen him struggle along the way. Perhaps the Banshee, who comes from Otherworld to wail - and she had been heard - before a McGrath dies, had spirited him across with the help of her Shee folk? Maybe his magical Druid ancestors? Even the great Mog Ruith himself, founder of the clan...

I lean against an old rowan tree under the vast silence of the starry sky, gazing at the thin sliver of a waxing moon.

"Now all the stars are shining, once it was difficult to see, but now all the

stars are shining and now they shine for me".
They twinkle happily for all of us. I muse as the stars look down as they looked down on Druidic Ireland fifteen centuries ago.

Has all the new religion ever since made any difference? It is true that our Druids had their own truths. They had no need for newcomers to tell them of any new philosophy or religion under the sun. The triple spiral at the heart of Newgrange images far off galaxies not seen with the naked eye. When asked any question they prefaced their answer with the words, "Not hard". They never had to pause to think. They knew, instantly. They could only have evolved as the aeons floated by into pure spirit, spirit that is still in the land, in the mounds, in the stones and in the sky and the stars above. They are still here. You will find them if you approach with respect, for they are in your very genes.

THE ARCHDRUID OF CASHEL.

The Druids, who united in a Society, occupied themselves with profound and sublime questions, raised themselves above human affairs, and sustained the immortality of the soul. "

- Ammianus Marcellinus,

Archbishop Myler McGrath of Cashel is the only man I can think of who was a Catholic and Protestant Archbishop at the same time. He had several wives and many sons and daughters, several of them Illegitimate. He provided for them. He made them all parish priests! Drinking a quart of whiskey a day, he lived to be 99. When he ran out of sons he appointed his daughters as parish priests, as many an old
druid before him did as well.

In fact the bold Myler was neither a Catholic nor a Protestant. He held both churches equally in contempt. He was a druid, the Chief Druid of Ireland of his time. Neither the Pope nor the Anglican authorities could do anything about it as he enjoyed the royal protection of the 'virgin queen', Elizabeth 1, who was madly in love with him above all other men of her realm and used to summon him over to London to her royal court several times every year. Myler was a direct descendant of the McGrath Druids who were Bards (Fili) of Limerick. He was from the North himself. Such was their prowess in prophecy, filiocht and music that the King of Munster demanded their services, so they arrived on the Rock of Cashel in neighbouring County Tipperary, thus establishing a long line of Archdruids of Munster. In time, at least two of them held the supreme appointment as Archdruid of Tara and Ireland.

During all the time he spent at the court of Elizabeth the Great we may well assume that he met her personal physician, the great alchemist, Doctor John Dee, famous for the Enochian Tables, and his magical assistant Edward Kelley, and that all three did at least 'swap notes'. One wonders indeed what they got up to, what mysteries they may have penetrated together, what Otherworlds they may have visited ...sometimes I see them bent upon the Great Work in a Tudor chamber under medieval London, peering into the future, perhaps the one we live in.

THE ABBOT OF LOUGH DERG

Along the way I have had several other notable ancestors such as the File Andrias MacCraith (Andrias McGrath), Druid-Bard of Limerick in the eighteenth century. Then there was the Abbot James McGrath, Prior of St. Patrick's Purgatory in Lough Derg, County Donegal. In 1497 he was ordered to seal off the cave there through which the Otherworld could be viewed. He refused and the king's men imprisoned him on the direct orders of the Pope. He was also a hereditary druid of Ireland and in the end he publicly refused to give up his druidic ways.

McGrath - MacCraith - MacRaith - MagRaith -MagRoith- MogRuith Mog Ruith - MacRoth - there is so much vowel change in the old scripts, with identical meaning. After being suppressed as druids, the McGrath clan became Fili and historians.

Now the very stones are speaking for our ancient druids to those who have inherited their genes. Many of the secrets are locked in the Irish language.

I would love to show you little books in Irish I have, such as Forbhais Droma Damhgaire and explain all the marvels to you, and so I will in due course. Briefly, in this little book you can actually see Druids in action, in particular my magical ancestor Mog Ruith. He is reputed to have learned his magic from Simon Magus and decapitated John the Baptist, so you can see why the Church might have suspicions about us fellows.

They could do nothing about old Myler McGrath, beyond slandering him as 'the scoundrel of Cashel' - but not within his earshot, as he was one of the finest swordsmen in Europe. Neither side, Catholic nor Protestant, could make any progress while he lived for 99 years. He was a personal friend of one of the finest patriots of the day, the great Irish chieftain Hugh O'Neill. The famous Irish writer Sean O'Faolain described Myler as the most level-headed man of his day. He was a druid and despised most of his contemporaries for their hypocrisy.

"Honour the gods, do no evil, be brave": for today's druids "Honour the gods" can mean one god or a thousand, or it can mean the Goddess or goddesses. It need not mean God in any literal sense. It can simply mean your 'higher power', your 'holy guardian angel', or your 'higher self'. There are druids who are agnostics and for them it can simply mean something like 'the Unknown' or Humanity.

THE HOLY MOUNTAIN OF THE DRUIDS

Croagh Patrick in County Mayo, the holiest mountain in Ireland, suddenly sprang into the news, majestic in all its splendid awe, on our television screens in the Spring of 1996.

There were photos of that majestic towering peak on the front pages of all the newspapers. Archaeologists had discovered three Druid ring forts on the summit of this, the most Catholic mountain in Ireland if not in the entire world. Yes, the Druids had been worshipping first atop this blessed Everest of Ireland. People were amazed by all the mass media coverage, staring agog at the sight of academics debating, and field archaeologists working in the full glare of the television cameras. I sat back in my old green Druid armchair and laughed. The Ancient Ones were at it again. The path to the summit is worn by the clambering bruised feet of thousands of Catholic pilgrims every year..   Many of the romanised Irish pilgrims stoop and stagger to the top, barefooted, during the last weekend in July.

Their efforts convert a Druidic first fruits festival into a Sunday Roman Catholic mass at the summit. The supplicants walk around Lecht Benin station on the mountain, then with a quick, surreptitious dab of the hand from rock cairn to head, they impart the rocks' power unto themselves.
The Reek, or Croaghpatrick as it is called, was in ancient times called Cruachan Aigle, perhaps from Aige -the act of celebrating festivals. It stands 762 meters high, a conical quartz-tipped mountain overlooking the Atlantic. Traditionally there are said to be 366 islands visible out in the ocean from the summit, enough, happily, for a druidic year and a day.

In ancient times people came every year at Lughnasadh to witness the mother goddess give birth. Barren women climbed up there hoping to participate, by way of sympathetic magic, in the birth process. Folklore describes the struggle of St. Patrick to overcome the Harvest God and the Earth Mother, although why anybody would oppose a good harvest and the bounty of the Earth only Rome knows.

The first cairn on the climb, where prayers are said, is known as Lecht Benin, 'bed of my boy' - the newly born infant of the goddess. William Makepiece Thackeray was there in 1840, when he discovered that the spirit of the goddess was alive and well at Croagh Patrick. After the ceremony on the mountain came the music, dancing and lovemaking at its foot. Fifty tents were set around 'a plain of the most brilliant green grass' where they sold 'great coarse damp looking bannocks of bread' ... a collection of pig's feet (crubeens), 'huge biscuits' and 'doubtful-looking ginger ale'. "There were also cauldrons containing water for 'tay', with other pots full of legs of mutton ...and the road home was pleasant; everybody was wet through but everybody was happy".

A few years later the laughter died. The Great Hunger, the famine of 1847, finally buried the people and all their happy druidic ways with them.

THE ARCHDRUID OF LOUGH GUR

Ten thousand years ago they landed in Ireland, the first people to watch the moon climb high between the Paps of Anu and see the sun go down over Galway Bay. The Sun Goddess Aine, Ana or Anu, Dana or Danu, with her sister Grian (the Sun), was worshipped mainly in the South West, in Munster. Aine Cli, Aine of the Light, the Beautiful, some worship her still.

Since before time began, and right up to the present time, there is an Archdruid on the sacred waters of Lough Gur. In summer on the night of the full moon the Archdruid always arranged for the people to bring their sick close to the lake so that the moonlight shone brightly upon them.

The old people called this night 'All Heal'. If the sick person was not better by the ninth day of the moon, he would then hear the Ceol Sidhe that Aine would sing to comfort the dying.

The sick person would then fall asleep to the music called The Banshee Wail, the whispering song of sleep which Aine's brother Fer Fi played.

He was a red-haired dwarf, and it was considered good luck to hear him laugh. He played only three tunes - Wail, Sleep and Laughter, on his three-stringed harp.

Aine gave birth at Lough Gur. Thus it is known locally as 'The Hatching Lake'. She gave birth to a horse, a black mare that became the property of the druid Dil. The druid gave it to his grandson, the landlord Fiachu, who in turn presented it to Fionn the warrior. Thus are ritually united the three representatives of the locality by the divine horse of social cohesion, born of the goddess. The courtesies of happy existence are fulfilled. The word 'Gur' can mean the pangs of pregnancy.

Knockadoon is the large rocky island that rises in the middle of Lough Gur, where Aine unites the hot sperm of sun and water. A picturesque intermingling of grey limestone cliffs, deciduous woodland and pasture, the remains of prehistoric habitats and stone circles dot its hilly surface. Knockadoon is the centre of a birth process involving Lough Gur as the womb of the goddess.

Despite some alterations of two centuries ago which joined Knockadoon to the mainland by two wide causeways, it is legitimate to understand the prehistoric island as a child of the lake - and, more important, as an image of Aine the mother goddess squatting in labour.

Everywhere Druidic art is centred on the birth act, linking human and divine nativity in an ageless island emerging from a lake. The sight of an island coming out of a ring of water was the inspiration for druids to concentrate monuments all around the lough. For, to the druid the land is alive, its bright heart beating as surely now as it did less than fifteen centuries ago. At such locations as Lough Gur, blessed because of its evocative attraction, the sacred life takes on a supernatural intensity personifying the goddess of the place, she who has always been here, birthing and nourishing throughout the aeons. Thus, Lough Gur and Knockadoon are Aine, mother and child, just as her breasts are the Paps of Anu further south. Here we have a goddess in childbirth straddling the land.
Lough Gur is the very antithesis of today's abortion culture, displaying for all time that Irish druidry was ever life affirmative.
Let us try to see the birth of Aine' s child, to catch a sight of the goddess in her birth chair. It is the Knockadoon Suiochan or Housekeeper's Chair. On this flat-topped limestone slab, Aine, the Supreme Housekeeper of Lough Gur is reputed to sit there at the old edge of the lake.

GEAROID IARLA

DeDanaan is now the collective name for many of the Irish nature gods. Aine or Dana is their goddess and belief in her has never died out. Certainly, she is widely regarded. If you should come across her magical son, Gearoid Iarla, be sure to speak to him as he can't speak until he is first spoken to. He was the Archdruid of Lough Gur during his lifetime. Many have worked in the job ever since. They are all very busy.

Wherever one travels in Munster the sacred is always close at hand, for the land and the people retain much of ancient sanctity. The great resources of a druidic past can be tapped afresh, for although religious perspectives may differ the sense of the sacred remains alive more out in the Irish landscape than anywhere else I know, though I have travelled far. The clear Munster air reminds us that our ancestors had no Irish word for 'superstition'. All matters of belief were treated seriously. They still are.

Chapter Five

The Mound of the Guardian

Were Canice and Colmcille one and the same?

As a young man it's said that Yeats slept overnight in the central chamber of Newgrange. Unfortunately, today you have to pay to get in, which goes towards the new interpretive centre. Fine, if they knew or could tell you anything about the druids. Surely the State authority that runs the place, Duchas, could employ druids?

Today's druids find it hard to suffer "unbelievers" running all our ancient places. The new centre is an eyesore as well. And you must accept a young guide and patiently listen,,,,,

My native city of Kilkenny in the southeast of Ireland wasn't Christianized until 597 AD. Two hundred years beforehand St. Kieran had preached to Carroll, King of Ossory, at his fort on the site of Kilkenny Castle, but to no avail. (St. Patrick's mission of 432 AD also failed in Kilkenny). King Carroll and his people weren't interested.

Kieran built a little wooden oratory and lived in it for a few years. We note well that Kieran was accorded full liberty to preach in freedom, as the other missionaries were, and to do as he wished by the king and the local druids.

There were no "hate speech" laws and jailings for speaking your mind back then.

After a few years of little progress in converting the locals he left. The mound, where the Druids lived, is only a couple of hundred yards away from my house in the centre of the city. It was the very last stronghold of the druids in Ireland.

Their end was not a peaceful one as the Christian army converged on ancient Kilkenny. St. Canice and his retinue who came to convert them at the close of the sixth century, ended up slaughtering the Druids. Canice was a son of the Chief Filidh of Donegal. The late great historian of Kilkenny, my friend John Bradley, believed that Canice and Colmcille were one and the same, and John was a distinguished Irish academic who lectured in ancient & medieval Irish history at Maynooth.

Dr. Bradley wrote that: " Padraig O'Riain has pointed out that, according to the old irish martyrologies, there are five saints with the name of Cainneach, and that at least three of these saints are the same individual, whose cult was practiced in Ulster by the end of the seventh century. The other two are unknown. More interesting however is O'Riain's analysis of the name Cainneach. The Irish liking for nicknames and pet names (formerly known as hypocorism) is an ancient one and O'Riain endeavours to show that the name Colum (as in Colum Cille, i.e. Columba) was transmuted into Cumma (and Mochumma), that Cumma became Conna , Conna became Conoc - and Conoc became Cainneach. O'Riain argument is that Cainneach is simply an alternative for Colum. While O'Riain's theory remains controversial, it is a reminder of the progress that has been made in the study of early Irish history during the twentieth century.

Great advances have occurred in the study of Old Irish and Hiberno-Latin, in the dating of manuscripts, in the preparation of critical editions as well as in archaeology and onomastics. The simple, uncritical attitudes of the nineteenth century no longer suffice in an era as complex as the study of early Irish history. Indeed this probably explains why there have been so few studies of early Irish saints, apart from Patrick, Columba and Columbanus- it now requires a great deal of knowledge and professional training to tackle the subject."

There is a magnificent Anglican cathedral on the mound, built circa 1250 AD under Norman supervision, but complete with a round tower from a ninth century church that stood previously on the site. Some hold that the round tower comes from an earlier time when such constructions were used as astronomical observatories. A major tourist attraction - both the fine Norman cathedral and the 108-foot high tower that visitors can ascend for a small donation of a couple of euros and view the 'Marble City and country for miles around.

The late Dean of Ossory, Dr. Norman Lynas, confirmed to me that there are crouch burials under the mound, with one discovered directly under the round tower. Irish Archdruidess Eileen Ennis wanted to excavate the entire site, but the Dean demurred. In fact our late great Kilkenny historian John Bradley confirms that "the tower was built on top of an earlier cemetery."

English Druidess Sandy Leigh from Blackpool, living in Ireland, was there, dowsed the ley lines and found naturally that the centre of the mound is on an intersection of ley lines. Almost everybody who has visited the site, including a party of teachers led by former college vice-principal Seamas MacCraith, has experienced the guardian spirit in one way or another.

We are dealing with the last major guardian spirit of the ancient Irish Druid Order. Although Canice and his soldiers killed the last Archdruid, they were unable to kill the guardian spirit, which is best described as a powerful energy form. Being an hereditary filidh magus, Canice was able to imprison the spirit in a force field. There is the official Christian history of Canice building a little round wooden church there, no bigger than your kitchen. We believe it was an enclosure that marked exactly where the guardian spirit was bound for fourteen centuries.

This was all brought home to us when some years ago an English occultist, living in Cork for over twenty years, came to Kilkenny to see me. Terence was a man of many talents, a Black Dan martial artist, a Ninja warrior, and electronics engineer.

He had been trained in magic and occult practice by no less maestro than the 'King of the Witches' himself - Alex Sanders. Terence became interested in Irish druidry, celebrating the summer solstice at Tara. Previously in England he had been involved in a psychic battle with an East London sorcerer called Owen Appleton, who claimed to be the 'Magister' of three London covens and 'Chief of the Order of the Knights of Taliesin'.

Terence insisted upon the superiority of his own strain of magic. He seemed to us to be the ideal candidate to make contact with the guardian spirit that he postulated was immanent in the mound, and he agreed. After his elaborate magical preparations the day came for Terence to try to establish contact. He walked up onto the mound with me. He approached the area the guardian occupies. Suddenly he panicked and ran. After five minutes or so of "earthing" himself around a tree trunk he came to, and spoke of a head-splitting roar he had experienced in a language he did not know, but he sensed the message - Get Out! - that 'blitzed' his mind. Obviously the guardian's 'radar' had sensed the presence of another powerful one and acted immediately in self-defence. I saw or felt nothing myself so I have to depend on his account. Terence later admitted that he approached with intent to control and dominate the spirit. During his stay in Kilkenny he was able to describe the guardian spirit as a succubus, deliberately created thus by the druids so it could survive through the centuries by feeding off the prayers, hymns and music of the worshippers in the church, later the cathedral, overhead. He located the guardian spirit as centering in the foundations of the cathedral seventy feet down where the old wooden ring fort lies buried in those foundations.

Dowsing by other sensitives subsequently appeared to confirm his findings, as did a multitude of other divinatory arts and sciences utilised over a three-year period. We were all intrigued and I seemed to 'feel' something there, scary and oppressive, though of course the suggestion was so strong it could have been my imagination.

A German dowser, knowing nothing about all of this, visited the cathedral one day. His divining rod, the cathedral sexton told me, went absolutely wild over two spots on the mound. The sexton showed me and I decided that the most important spot was under the great window in the east wall near the high altar. I subsequently came across a druid stone, which forms part of the outer surface of this east wall, with Druidic astrological symbolism engraved upon it, which I deciphered. The late sexton, George Wilde, a close friend of mine in life, always swore that the cathedral was haunted, "but by a good spirit".

Another Irish Druid visited the mound together with his associates from the Gaeltacht Grove of Druids.

He felt the energy course through his veins, as all the others did, and described it as a nexus of powerful telluric force. Many others, including non-Druids we have introduced there, have felt the power on the mound.

Terence brought me to a vantage point from where he could see the aura of the spirit, which extended way out through the east window, a pulsating purple trying to burst through a boundary, which looked like a golden elastic band, he described. He told me that the spirit was male and that the reason it was struggling to get free over the centuries was that it would never be satisfied until it united with its twin, which is female, over in Glastonbury, directly to the east. He told me that they would lovingly unite, if freed.

After all, fourteen centuries 'solitary confinement' is enough and we had begun to actually empathise with the 'loneliness' of the guardian spirit. So, finally Terance broke the spell of the Christian Canice and freed the guardian. He is quite free to come and go now, Terence told us, twixt this and Otherworld but seems content to remain in and around his old habitat of fourteen centuries. Institutionalisation?

We think not. He just prefers to stay with us here in Kilkenny, we like to think. Living as I do on the adjoining mound, Terence remarked that I hadn't moved very far in fourteen centuries of re-incarnation! Well-known Celtic Christian Gillies MacBain of Crannagh Castle, Templemore, County Tipperary, simply remarked that St. Canice's Cathedral is on an ancient Druidic site. How did the last Archdruid of Ireland and his entourage happen to be living there in the sixth century, and not at Tara or Cashel or Newgrange, on top of Croagh Patrick or at Lough Derg, or some other well-known druidic place? For the very reason that such sites were so well known to the Christian authorities of the period, these remaining druids were on the run for their lives. The mound at Kilkenny, although inhabited since 2,000 BC, was not so well known to the armies led by monks around Ireland seeking out druids.

At this time even the word Druid was outlawed. Canice was sent to the mound at Kilkenny to terminate the last Archdruid and take over the last Druid stronghold in sixth century Ireland. Over fourteen centuries later we like to think that he wasted his time.

In his article "Canice and Kilkenny" published by John Bradley in the book, "Kilkenny Through The Centuries" edited by John Bradley & Michael Dwyer and published by Kilkenny Borough Council in 2009, John Bradley continued:

"Many other great miracles were performed by the Lord Jesus Christ through his holy servant Canice but they are not written down here because of the need to be concise. He raised eight people from the dead, he enabled the blind to see, the deaf to hear, the dumb to talk, and he rid many places of demons. His other virtues, of which there were many, have been omitted because of the need to be brief. As the day of his own death approached, his body became weak with sickness but he refused to take communion from the hands of any of his monks. Instead he said: "The Lord wishes to send another holy man to me , named Fintan, and from him I will accept the body of Christ." Then St. Fintan Moeldubh [Fintan of Clonenagh, Co. Laois], sent by the Lord, came to him and accepting the Eucharist from his hand at the monastery of Achadh Bo, on 11th October, St. Canice went happily to the Lord Jesus Christ, to whom is all honour and glory for ever and ever, amen." (the normal scholarly rendition of his name

is Cainneach - notes, Bradley.).
"So ends the Life of Canice from whom Cill Chainnigh, anglicised as Kilkenny, 'the church of Canice' gets its name,

It does not tell us the year of Canice's death. (placed variously between 598 and 603 AD. from the stories linking Canice and Columba (Colum Cille) of Iona, later annalists would have concluded that they were contemporaries and since it was known that Columba died in 597 AD , a date in or about that time would have been appropriate for Canice. Our dates of 598, 599, 600 or 603 for the death of Canice are based on nothing more substantial than this."

However, Bradley goes on to explain that whereas the relationship between Canice and Kilkenny "is little understood and little written about", this was not always so:

"In the eighteenth and nineteenth centuries the early Irish saints were much fought over and several local antiquaries interested themselves in the lives of the saints. Edward Ledwich (1737-1823), the author of the first published history of Kilkenny (1791), was rector of Aghaboe, and could claim to be the successor of Canice there, but famously declared that all the Irish saints , including St. Patrick, were fictional. Canice, he maintained, "was an imaginary personage"; the lives of the saints were 'monkish fictions', and it was the duty of the (Anglican) Church 'under the fostering care of Britain'(as he put it) to cleanse religion of such superstition. He was not alone in this view, which was, perhaps, somewhat sectarian in Ledwich's case. It reflected the rationalist approach of historians like his contemporary, Edward Gibbon (1737-94) who had famously and notoriously) debunked many of the saints of the early Christian church and, in particular, the 11,000 virgin martyrs of Cologne.

"Ireland has long claimed to be the island of saints. "Island of Saints" is the very phrase used by Arnold le Poer at Kilkenny in 1324 when he denounced Bishop Richard Ledrede for daring to suggest that Alice Kyteler was a heretic. "Don't you know", he said, "that this is the island of saints; heretics are unknown here? " The problem for the scholar, however, is that there are far too many saints per head of population and the stories about them stretch credulity. The same names occur over and over again. There are 27 St. Finians, 25 St Senans, 30 St. Cronans, 12 St. Bridgets, 10 St Gobans, 58 St Mochuas, 43 St Molaises and Colmans innumerable. The total ages of one group of 10 saints amount to 3090 years; several dozen saints are remembered because they had leprosy, others because they were bald, or thin, or one-eyed, or because they were stammerers; and all of the saints were aristocrats and related to each other. (many were in fact druids and druidesses - author).

"In his book (Hubert) Butler argued that the saints were ancestor deities who were subsequently christianised ... indeed in the light of Hubert Butler's doubts , the first question that has to be asked is, "did St. Canice exist?"

And now, today, the late great Hubert Butler is somewhat supported by the view of Padraig O'Riain, Professor of Old Irish at University College Cork, that Canice is in fact one and the same person as Columba of Iona - still a controversial view that I share here a couple of hundred yards from the awesome cathedral of his name in Kilkenny. Were Canice and Colmcille one and the same? That is academically a valid open question now.

Chapter Six

The Lost Wisdom of the Druids

The Persians, I think, have men called Magi ...the Egyptians their priests ... and the Indians their Brahmins. On the other hand, the Celts have men called Druid ...who concern themselves with divination and all branches of wisdom. And without their advice even kings dared not resolve upon nor execute any plan, so that in truth it was they who ruled, while the kings, who sat on golden thrones and fared sumptuously in their palaces, became mere ministers of the Druids' will.

- Dion Chrysostom, 354 - 407 AD

The ancient druids often 'spoke in a riddle', leaving it to the recipient to work out the received wisdom. Traces of the druidic oral lore, as rediscovered by us in an Irish-speaking Gaeltacht area, has several references to An Fuinneamh, or The Energy, meaning the telluric force of earth energies. This earth energy is not unidirectional, but pulses back and forth along the major ley lines in a similar way to alternating current, although it has a much slower frequency.

The Irish word Nem, or Neamh, can mean nothing or 'nothingness' on the one hand, or 'Heaven' on the other hand. From 'Nemed' we have the Nemedians, a caste of high magical Greco-Druids. The student is entering in from the 'nothingness' of the outer world, to be initiated in stages.

Ar nAthair ata ar Neamh begins the Lord's Prayer in Irish - the translators certainly knew their druidry! So too did Jesus, an Essene, when he replied to the disciples in the Gnostic Gospel;

"Have you discovered then the beginning, that you look for the end? For where the beginning is, the end will be. Blessed is he who will take his place in the beginning; he will know the end and will not experience death."

Resurrection of the spirit during our own lifetimes is the clear implication of his message, or, in druidic wisdom, passage through all the initiatory stages to find the kingdom within. Thus the soul is freed to evolve higher. Druidry has so much in common with the gnostics too, or is it the other way around?

In English we have Beltane, which is a Druidic festival, given different meanings up to now. Here at last I give the real meaning of this festival. Beltane is the English corruption of the Irish word Bealtaine.

Beal-Taine = Mouth-Fire and Beal-Taine = Mouth-Saga. Of course! A double initiation, when under the first quarter of the Moon the student was initiated. He or she was given the Fire in the mouth to intone the magical words in divination and consecrated as a Faith (pronounced 'Fawee' and meaning a diviner-Druid or prophetess) - and from where the Irish surname FAHY comes.. Beal means 'Mouth' in Irish- druidry has never had anything to do with the Canaanite God Baal.

From Bealtaine onwards the newly initiated Faith (in English, Ovate) was busy in preparation for the great solar festival of the Summer Solstice, Midsummer Day, when that great festival and Council was held on the royal hill of Tara. The newly consecrated Faith had to train for a further nine years (3 x 3) to become a druid, attended by three Daltai (Students).

Again we see that the festival of imbolc is dated according to the phase of the moon. Imbolg was always held on the sixth day of the new moon (1 x 2 x 3). Aspirants were initiated as Daltai into the Order of Druids at Imbolc.

The Festival of Lughnasadh, under the full moon, was the time for consecration of those druids who were now fully qualified and passed by the Masters of the Order. The festival celebrated the solar activity of the sun upon which all life on Earth (and climate change) depends. There was, of course, the secondary aspect of celebrating an early harvest or festival of first fruits

The Festival of Samhain was the highpoint of the Druidic year, the time when the gateways between this and Otherworld opened - naturally under the last quarter of a waning moon. It was not the end of the Celtic year. That happened and was precisely measured at Newgrange at Midwinter, at the death and rebirth of the sun. This was the time when the greatest of druids were consecrated as masters. There was no fixed amount of years to achieve the grade of Master Druid, but it generally took thirty years in the Order, the period of one complete orbit of Saturn around the sun, or a Saturn return.

It took 19 years to become a full Druid of Ireland, based on the Metonic cycle of 18.6 years. We know of several ways in which the ancient druids were able to utilise the telluric force of earth energies. Many tons of different stones were moved hundreds of miles, even across rivers, lakes and seas. The druids were the engineers at either end of the ley lines, manipulating the pure pulsating energies. For instance, druids would have supervised the high points, the stations of the major ley line across Ireland, from Valentia Island to the Isle of Mona, their Holy Island of Holyhead. The stones moved along these major lines at the exact planetary time, when the forces were right, according to the relative energies of the solar wind and the planets as they moved into a precise pattern. The Druids intoned the magic words of command and the stones moved along the leys to their destinations. As one line ended, say at Mona, there was a 'junction' where another leyline took over the task - just like trains along the tracks. These stones did not touch the ground. They hovered across the land and sea. The telluric force was used for actual flight through the air too. Thus the legends, for instance of Mog Ruith flying over what is now Lake Lucerne in Switzerland. The words of command are inherent in words still in the Irish language.

HY BRASIL A REAL PLACE

The ancient Irish regarded Breasail as the High King of the World. He built Bare Breasail in Leinster, a huge fortress. He lived in the West in a land known as Hy Brasil, which was the legendary Atlantic island, said to be visible every seven years, when anybody who looked upon it would die.

Ruairi O'Flatharta (Rory Flaherty) in writing his A Geographical Description of the West of Iar Connaught (London 1684) tells of a man called O 'Ley ("of the ley-line") who claimed he was kidnapped and taken to the fabled island. The name Hy-Brasil actually appears on maps as a real place. The Genoese cartographer A. Dalerto, in 1325 AD, placed it in latitudes of 44 degrees southwest of Ireland. Hy-Brasil was so real in medieval European minds that when South America was discovered they thought at first that they had come across the legendary land and named it Brasil or Brazil.

A tower of crystal stood on Tory Island, off the northwest coast of Ireland, at the end of yet another cross-country ley line. The Druids used instruments and structures of crystal to control, purify and direct the telluric force of earth energies.

THE LOST SECRETS

The Roman conqueror of Gaul, Julius Caesar, was responsible for the loss of thousands of scrolls in the Druid College of Bibractis at what is now Autun in France. Numerous treatises on philosophy, medicine, astronomy and the other sciences perished there, as did hundreds of volumes of the sacred wisdom later under St. Patrick in Ireland. Our ancientDruids were as proficient in astronomy as the priests of Egypt and Sumer. The computations of the Stonehenge alignments, made by Professor Gerald S. Hawkins, have disclosed a precise knowledge of the solstices, equinoxes and the ability to predict eclipses by the builders of those megaliths around 2000 BC.

The complexity of the Stonehenge astronomical tradition shows a development of some thousands of years.

Did this science develop locally in the British Islands or was it 'imported' from another centre of advanced civilisation, the mystical land westward beyond the Pillars of Herakles? It appears that the spiritual and scientific impulse in ancient times came in upon these British Islands from somewhere out there in the western ocean and travelled eastwards across Europe, the middle east, Asia and into India and China. One thing is strikingly clear from their workings - the ancient ones had a clear concept of geometry and astronomy and their work was thoroughly scientific.

Computers before Christ!

Surprises from the Ancients are now the order of the day. The ancient Greeks, whose DeDanaans and Nemedians came to Ireland, with Parthalonians here before them, were in possession of objects called celestial spheres. According to Cicero, Marcus Marcellus of Syracuse in Sicily possessed such a sphere that demonstrated the motions of the sun, the moon and the planets. Cicero assures us that the machine that was a very ancient invention, and that a similar astronomical model was in the Temple of Virtue at Rome. Thales of Miletus in the sixth century BC and Archimedes in the third century BC were the constructors of these mechanical devices.

The National Archaeological Museum of Greece in Athens possesses corroded fragments of a metallic object found by sponge-divers near the island of Antikythera in 1900 AD. The complex dials and gears of the mech-

anism are unlike any artifact from ancient Greece.
From the inscription and the amphorae found along with it, a date of approximately 65 BC was ascribed to the machine.

The museum registered the machine as an astrolabe until 1959 when Dr. Derek J. De Solla Price, an English scientist working for the Institute of Advanced Study at Princeton, New Jersey, identified it as an ancestor of our computer. "It appears that this was indeed a computing machine that could work out and exhibit the motions of the sun and moon and probably also of the planets", he wrote in Natural History, March 1962. The purpose of the gadget was to save tedious astronomical calculations. He formed the conclusion that the Antikythera Computer had changed all our ideas about the history of science; "Finding a thing like this is like finding a jet plane in the Tomb of Tutankhamen", he told a meeting in Washington.

A few years later druidry was taken very seriously indeed with the momentous discoveries about Stonehenge and Newgrange. After a critical study of Stonehenge the British astronomer Gerald Hawkins, Professor of Boston University, concluded it might have astronomical significance.
Stonehenge, as we know by now, was completed by 2000 BC. It originally consisted of a 29-meter ring of 25-ton uprights and horizontal slabs, called the Sarsen circle, inside of which stood five trilithons or archways.

Taking his observations from the centre of Stonehenge, Professor Hawkins became convinced that aligning archways, stones and holes with the sun or moon when on the horizon, was one of the purposes of this enigmatic structure.

Returning to America with accurate charts of Stonehenge, Hawkins fed the data into a computer, which produced the results that Stonehenge itself had been a computer! Professor Hawkins estimated that the building of this megalithic computer was an effort comparable with the U.S. Space programme.

The energies of one person in a thousand in the U.S.A. are absorbed in the space programme at its height. Considering the population of Britain four thousand years ago, the proportion was similar in the construction of Stonehenge.

We are now beginning to recognise that the ancient Druids, than ever previously thought possible, knew a much higher level of science and technology. We are beginning to turn increasingly to the tradition of a golden age rather than a savage, primitive past, to acknowledge that our ancestors were simply brilliant.

The history, mythology and sacred books of most races support this assertion. Philo of Alexandria wrote two millennia ago:

"By reason of the constant and repeated destructions by water and fire, the latter generations did not receive from the former the memory of the order and sequence of events."

In the Timaeus Plato records the words of an Egyptian Priest:

"There have been, and there will be again, many destructions of mankind."

"When civilisation is destroyed by natural calamities you have to begin all over again as children", said the High Priest of Egypt to Solon.

The population of the world, at the time of the Roman destruction of European Druidry two thousand years ago, was 250 million. At the time of the construction of Stonehenge, two thousand years before that, the world population was only ten millions.

The story of Atlantis, as told by Plato, came to him from the priests of Neith in Sais through Solon:

"I am what has been, what is and what shall be," the priests maintain they were told, and they kept the chronicles of history through thousands of years.

Herodotus admitted that he was unable to reveal certain mysteries, which he had learned from the Temple of Neith.

Probably for the very same reason we cannot reveal certain Druidic mysteries, because people would first have to know the very basis upon which these mysteries can be understood, and this takes many years of hard study and discovery.

Those earliest and most ancient of the druids came into these islands from the western ocean, they also travelled through the Straits of Gibraltar, and

in the other direction reached the Americas.
They came into the land of Ireland, went on to Britain and Gaul, spread throughout Europe on an earlier Druidic mission of advancing civilisation. Culture bearers of the Greeks, they went into the land of Isis and there wrought and raised wonders. They excelled across the land of Sumer and were great astronomers along the Tigris, Euphrates and Ur of the Chaldees. "Yes, the divine ones were here and they are gone..."
Thus spake Zarathustra...

THE BOYNE VALLEY

The entire necropolis was built to an exact astronomical order, providing a form of calendar as well as a magical centre of worship and sacred rule. The obvious intelligence, knowledge and talent of the Boyne Valley elite place them well above all others of the time. No race of contemporary Europe even comes close to matching them. All an Irish government, that included the Irish Green party, could do in recent years is drive a big ugly motorway through the sacred Tara valley - Ireland went bust after that!

The clay tablets of Sumeria date from about 5500 years ago and the ancient Irish inscriptions can be dated before that. Not for the first time does it appear that civilisation set out from the shores of the Atlantic, from the Boyne Valley of Ireland. And not for the first time does it seem to be one of the least studied civilisations in the ancient world.

The earliest known system of writing is the Sumerian cuneiform writing of 3500 BC, with records discovered six kilometers northeast of Ur in Mesopotamia - 'Ur of the Chaldees' now in Iraq. According to C.H. Gordon, the earliest known European texts are three unintelligible clay tablets from Tartaria in Transylvania, dating from the start of the third millennium BC which show early literacy in the Balkans that may be connected with Sumeria.

No connection anywhere in the world has been found for the Irish inscriptions in the Boyne Valley, the earliest in the whole wide earthly world.

For long before 3500 BC the ancient Irish had their calendar as seen on two large stones at Knowth. The Boyne Valley archaeological excavations, together with careful recording and painstaking analysis of the incised markings on over two hundred megaliths there, have revealed one of the most important discoveries in the prehistory of the world. The Knowth calendar illustrates the high intelligence, abilities, talents and skills of this unique group among the most ancient people of Ireland. An analysis of the incised designs on the kerbstones is clear evidence of that considerable logic and skill. The mathematical form of the calendar points towards a formal philosophy.

On a Knowth kerbstone I see a wavy line with twenty nine bends. This is taken as the number of days in a moon's cycle of phases, the days in a lunar month. The actual precise period is 29.503, as we know it from our computers today.

THE LOUGHCREW CALENDAR STONE.

The Loughcrew area is forty kilometers west of the Boyne Valley. The eastern hill has a stone circle near its crest - the references describe it as 'cairn X'. A ring of eight stones surrounds the centre stone which is about one meter wide. The concave side of this centre stone faces north and the symbols inscribed on it are similar to those at Knowth.

The story it tells is similar to the Knowth account. The similarity of the two designs at Knowth and Loughcrew points towards a similar philosophy for two distant communities.

The simple inscription on Cairn F stone Cl at Loughcrew shows nine vertical columns of hoops', of upside-down 'u' figures or simple 'n' shapes. The insignificant difference of three days in five years hardly detracts from the Loughcrew stone assertion of 3500 BC!

The declaration on Loughcrew stone Cl is obviously a public statement of the relationship between the two calendars. The Loughcrew calendar stone also supports the legitimacy of the Coligny calendar three and a half millennia before it was uncovered from the earth at Coligny near Bourg-en-Bresse in France.

THE COLIGNY CALENDAR.

The Coligny Calendar is a first-century bronze tablet which gives us archaeological evidence of Druidic computation of days and months. Originally measuring 5 feet by 3.5 feet, but now greatly fragmented, it is engraved with a calendar of 62 lunar months and two additional or intercalary months.

The language is Gaulish Celtic, but the lettering is Roman. Each month is divided into two halves; the propitious half of the waxing moon indicated by the word MAT (Irish 'Math' meaning good) and the unpropitious half of the waning moon indicated by the letters ANM (ANMAT meaning 'not good'). Many of the inscriptions are obvious abbreviations.

The Coligny Calendar is reckoned in nights followed by days, which we know from Caesar's observation and from other sources to have been the Celtic method of reckoning.

However, even the apparently indisputable evidence of the Coligny Calendar leads to controversy and uncertainty, as is so often the case with the Druids. Robert Graves dismisses the Coligny Calendar as not truly druidic: he clearly states that in his view the tablet represents a stage in the Romanization of Gaul, when the Celts tried to please their Roman masters by adopting foreign calendrical systems.

Crucial to his argument is the fact that the calendar is based on lunations, that is, periods of twenty-nine and a half days, rather than on the 'lunar months' of twenty eight days to which he subsequently devotes so much attention in his very best book, The White Goddess. Obviously Robert Graves did not know of the Loughcrew Calendar Stone bearing silent witness on a lonely Irish hillside to the Coligny Calendar since 3500 BC. It is just like all those modern Wiccans who mistakenly hold that The Druidic Year ends and begins at Samhain. It does not! Newgrange is long and silent testimony to the fact that the Druidic Year ends and starts precisely at the Midwinter Solstice.

Our modern Western calendar is a solar one. The awkward additional hours, roughly a quarter of a day, that are left over at the end of a year, are accommodated by the system of making every fourth year a leap year of 366 days. The solar calendar is child's play compared to the lunar calendar, that is, the system of reckoning the year by the waxing and waning of the moon. Yet many of the world's religions are based on the lunar calendar. This is why the feasts and festivals of many religions and nations, particularly the Eastern ones, appear on different dates from year to year in our solar, or Western, calendar. The best-known movable feast in the Christian calendar is Easter, being the first Sunday after the first full moon after the Spring equinox each year.

There are four separate but related movements in the skies, as seen from

Earth, which would have been apparent to ancient man: the rotation of the stars; the movements of the brighter planets, Jupiter, Saturn, Venus, Mercury and Mars; the movements of the sun; the movements of the moon. Stars and the 'wandering stars' called planets caused immense difficulties to the Ancients. The apparent movements of the sun and the moon seemed far more obvious, easier to comprehend and to accommodate in a mathematical model. Even so there were complications that could only be
understood by close observation over relatively long periods of time. The complication with the sun is that the positions of its rising and setting varies with the seasons. In winter when the days are short, it rises and sets further towards the south. In summer, when the days are long, it rises further to the north, climbs higher and stays longer in its journey across the sky, and sets further to the north.

The complication with the moon is more subtle and it requires very careful observation. The moon returns to the same position in the sky approximately every nineteen years. Most people in today's western society have never seen a single moonrise, let alone made the countless observations ancient man had to make before attempting to reach an understanding of these celestial movements. When 40 would have been ripe old age, precise astronomical observations and recordings over a period
of nineteen years seem remarkable. Our time, calculated with atomic precision today, could not run on the Coligny Calendar - but the druid world could, and did.

The Craft of the Druid

Chapter Seven

Druidcraft

Druidcraft describes the principles and practices of druidry in purifying the land, healing the people, and connecting with Otherworld. Druidcraft also teaches the various divinations known to druidry and it does this in depth over many years. It is all very fine to visualise the wisdom of the Druids in terms of some hard-and-fast "nuggets of wisdom" consisting of wise saws and sayings, which they probably had, more than likely in poetic form so as to more easily remember them. In any case it is the outlook, the attitude, the approach, the philosophy of the druids in practice, which is so important.

Druidry is more grounded. Rather than total faith, as Christianity has, in an afterlife, druidry doubts and always searches for real connections with life after death. Druidry never works by faith alone. If druidry is to be classified as a religion, then at least let it be a thinking person's religion. This is where many of the modern books on Druidry are "falling apart at the seams. They introduce rituals and ceremonies that quite frankly never were. Of course these things are attempted reconstructions of druidry, attempts by people who have seized on a good idea - druidry itself - to begin with. Druidry is the only belief system I know that teaches people to live life to the full, to enjoy wine, sex and song today for tomorrow we die - that was most certainly a theme of Irish druidry. It still is.

As a spiritual discipline Druidry does have its finer teachings. It has also accrued to itself a fine 'occult' component in recent centuries since its revival.

Let's leave all those magnificent ceremonial magicians to their ongoing battles on the astral while we get back to the basics of druidry, which can get highly advanced, if you let it get out of hand. Now, we have to admit that people are fed up to their back teeth with religion, especially with the religions of the western world. Druidry is also under the microscope as I write. What people want, first and foremost, out of any religion, is an absolute assurance that they are going to survive death. Almost all religions have given this assurance at some time or another, and then went on to dodge this central promise for the rest of their existences. Irish druidry differs. It does not give any such assurances and certainly no guarantees. In fact druidry continually queries and questions all the other religions at every hand's turn about this crucial issue of human survival after death. We are not lightly put off.

The Irish word Druidecht is translated as 'magic, that is, the magic of the craft of Druidry. 'Druth' is 'madman' in the sense of inspired madness or inspiration. In Sanskrit the word 'drus' means 'tree' and 'duru' means 'woodland'. In Lithuanian 'doire' means 'oak' while in Irish the same word means 'grove'. Door is 'drws' in Welsh, 'dorus' in Gaelic, 'Daras' in Cornish and 'durys' in Lithuanian. 'Druidim' is the verb 'I shut' in Gaelic, so we gather that the root from which the word 'Druid' comes from is widespread throughout the Indo-European world and that it is powerfully connected with oaks, groves and the opening and closing of ways. In Irish Drui is 'Druid' and Draoi is 'magician' or mage.

The word Druid may also come from the intensive Dru, meaning Strong and the root Vid, meaning see, combining to produce Druvid, meaning Strong Seer. Certainly this is one clear function of a druid.
In Irish, druid is in fact the plural of drui.

I agree too with the suggestion of Peter Berresford Ellis, the well-known writer and authority on the Celts, himself a considerable Irish druid, that the druids were present in the ancient world from an earlier time before the arrival of the Celts and that they continued to be active for far longer than is generally accepted, but not always under the name Druid. That name was gradually applied in ancient times to the wise ones of the West, and in later times the Church outlawed it under the penalty of death. That the druids were in the land long before the Celts now seems certain. Some authors call them proto-druids. For obvious reasons I refer to them as Atlantean druids. As for druidic survival right into our present time, hereditary druids dotted in our ones and twos around the fringes of the Celtic world attest to this fact.

An accusation often levelled against our ancient druids is that they practiced human sacrifice. There is not a scintilla, not a single shred of evidence to support this hoary old gem of the 'bogey-man' propagandists. It is also telling that the viciously anti druidic monks of the sixth and seventh centuries never made this allegation. They would have gladly done so if it had in fact happened, if there was even a single instance of such practice. In all the long history of Ireland there is not one single instance of human sacrifice so for to suggest it happened at all is to demean our history, culture and high international standing as one of the most civilised nations on the face of the Earth. Only a fool or a charlatan would make such a base unfounded allegation.

There is indeed one instance in the Irish Celtic Christian hagiography where the great St. Colmcille is accused of the human sacrifice of his disciple Oran of Iona, and this is still alleged to the present day.
Colmcille was a leading light of the Bardic Order of the Fili, while Oran was a fully-fledged druid. To the relief of the millions of followers in the world today of this great man of God, Colmcille, the entire episode can be explained as a symbolic working of Druidcraft.

There was no idolatry either among the druids. The druid mind does not run that way. It was Christianity that introduced human figures in stone, called statues, and it still keeps them. The alleged 'idols' were important stones incorporated in the landscape, as also described in the Druidcraft section of this book. Our ancient druids reckoned the soul to be coterminous with the body - but we question even our own venerable predecessors, wondering if they are correct? Or does the body house the soul at all? Is the soul somewhere 'up there', an alter ego halfway across the universe? What druidry needs right now, more than any other thing, is for people to come and help in our search for the soul. In short, we need fresh input. As a good man who calls himself King Arthur says: "We druids are here for a purpose. Until we find out what that purpose is we shall continue to fight for truth, honour and justice." And it is in this spirit that we now pass on to explore the system of Druidcraft.In doing so we have to find a powerpoint to connect up some power for our experiments in Druidcraft. That powerpoint is called dowsing, the plug is called a pendulum, and the cable is a dowser.

THE PENDULUM AND THE STARS

Mention a dowser and people will immediately picture a rather rustic old fellow in Wellington boots trudging around a field dowsing for water. This is a true picture and it works. But it is far from the whole picture, as that old dowser will tell you. The chances are that the man or woman using a pendulum or divining rods today is actually young, with a university degree to boot.

Academics are coming around to the fact that dowsing works. They can't explain it but they know it works. It may come as a surprise to you that you can dowse too. Just hold a short pendulum in whatever hand you like for a couple of minutes, and what a surprise you will get when that pendulum starts gyrating!

This is evidence of the latent 'psychic' power dormant in everybody, and this power is one of the real pointers we have to the spirit, the soul - and the afterlife, one of the few 'proofs'. I advisedly use the word 'psychic', because what the majority of people think is unusual or paranormal I know to be quite normal.

Everybody is to some extent 'psychic' but few people realise they are. Everybody I have ever introduced to the pendulum has reacted with delight, dowsing for hours and days on end. Naturally people dowse to find the winning numbers in the national lottery and such like, and even if you don't win, it's all fabulous fun. Take off your necklace and start dowsing right now. Get all your friends and family involved - pass the pendulum around as it whirls and whizzes with power.

Get a little book on dowsing and divining - there are several of them on the market, all inexpensive, and all equally good. Dowsing has many important applications, in diagnostics for instance.

You can dowse for anything - oil, precious metals, ancient artifacts or old coins buried in the earth. When you get to 'know' how to use it, with a lot of practice to get the 'feel' for it all, the hazel twig can be more telling than the latest electronic metal detector, because the dowsing twig 'knows' through your Being exactly what it is looking for - the electronic gadget doesn't.

Yet I still encourage use of all the latest 'state-of-the-art' electronic equipment in psychic questing because many people will find it easier to use.

The vital telluric force of earth energies is distributed across the Earth in what have become known, in what I think to be a lovely terminology, as Earth Stars. All these Earth Stars are then connected together in a matrix, somewhat resembling a beehive structure. Earth Stars are not flat circles. They are globes, emerging half above the surface of the land, and half below. They are invisible to everyday normal sight. Clairvoyants and druids who are trained to use our 'psychic' powers, can see them. They are a kaleidoscope of colour and vibrating energy, not still but surging, whirling and twirling in lovely harmonies. They can be 'rediscovered' by walking the land with a dowsing rod or pendulum, whichever suits you.

Using the pendulum can be awkward out there in the open due to the wind, and the only way it can be employed satisfactorily is to wear a robe or cloak (coming back into fashion again!) to shield it from the wind as you move around. You can sit down and gradually plot out your findings on paper. This is referred to as dowsing the ley lines.

When you get home you can transcribe them onto actual maps. It is time consuming, but is a fascinating pastime, and with the dedication, say, of a fisherman, you can gradually map out the 'run' of the ley lines in and around your own locality over a period of time. Try it the next fine day you are out, say, in your own back garden.

Believe me, after your very first exercise of dowsing the ley lines you won't wait to try out your new-found skills on that ancient cathedral, ruined abbey or old mound nearby. There are the most excellent earth energy societies working on many such projects all over Britain and healing the scars in the Earth. At the time of writing I do not know of the existence of any specific earth energy society in Ireland.

Some of our Druids go out in the land from time to time, sometimes for weeks on end. I hear of groups in the Dublin Mountains, down around Cork and in the Slieve Bloom hills of County Laois. The very first task of any earth energy society in Ireland would be to try to somehow heal the mortally wounded Hill of Tailteann, destroyed some years back by a madwoman on a JCB as a result of corruption in the local County Council. Tara Valley is 'red raw' too after rape for a motorway by the last FF-Green party government was finished with it. There are druids today convinced that the 'mi adh', the bad luck, sprung back on them threefold with the collapse of the Irish economy. We druids call it the Threefold Law of Return.

When using a short pendulum out in the open you must get down on your knees, right down close to the ground, and 'walk' along on your knees, with your cloak protecting the gyrating pendulum from the wind.

Any decent dowsing book- they're in your local public library- will show you how to cut the hazel twig, and how to make up a set of dowsing rods from wire coat hangers.

The late Commander Clive Beadon DFC, in his work as a professional diviner, came up with the clearest description of Earth Stars available, so it is best to quote the master:

" The surface of the Earth is covered by an interlocking pattern of energy lines, the nature of which is not fully understood: they do not appear to be either electrical or magnetic but they can be identified by a dowser. The pattern shows as a six-pointed star within a circle, each unit touching the next and linked together by the major energy line running through the centres. The basic colours of the lines of the patterns are white, red, black and blue.

"In areas away from man's activities the patterns can be traced in their balanced repeating shapes, but where they have been damaged, fragmented lines are generated and it is near these points that disharmony occurs. To a dowser these lines have the characteristic that they show as black and carry the apparent information of being water. It is probably the origin of traditional black leys and black streams. These patterns, sometimes like the acupuncture lines of the human body, are normally in balance, but they can be diverted or destroyed and the resulting disharmony and uneasiness affects people in the area. Since we all have the dowsing sense, although we may not be aware of it, we can all be affected in varying degrees by such disturbances. The effect of such damage is being noted by an increasing number of interested people and there seems to be a growing correlation between their presence and inexplicable tension, unease and illness.

(Earth Stars - Clive Beadon assisted by Geoffrey King).

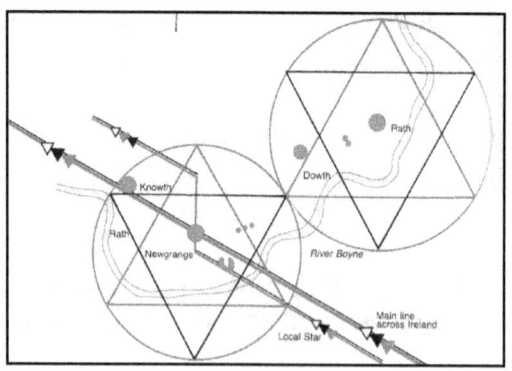

THE SPIRALS OF TRANQUILITY

The good news is that Clive Beadon went on to construct an instrument called The Spirals of Tranquillity to heal and restore earth energy sites, which have been damaged by man. This instrument consists of crystals of the quartz family set in a specific pattern inside a copper spiral. The copper, encircling and energising the crystals, creates a new telluric force field that forms a vortex, which whirls out into a globe of over two hundred yards radius and recreates the Earth Star to perfection.

Stone circles were built over subterranean water crossings. This was one of the origins of stone circles and ring forts. The underground water crossing is the source of an upward energy spiral and the radius of the stone circle was calculated to be the same as the depth of the water crossing directly underneath. The long pendulum, as described in The Complete Book of Dowsing and Divining by Peter Underwood, generally measured this.

Use of the long pendulum - it resembles the action of paying out a fishing line - will give you the most accurate underground readings of all. You can put one together for a Euro or two, by adapting an old fishing rod. It's the way the ancient druids used a pendulum.

CONTROLLING URBAN CHAOS

The situation seems hopeless, the earth energies are all black and negative here where you live, it's alright for that druid to be pontificating...

Well there is hope and you can remain living in the middle of that dirty old smog ridden, traffic-congested city with electric and telephone cables and even power pylons crossing and criss-crossing all around you - although the latter can cause cancer and brain tumours. Mobile phones cause both - and Alzeimer's disease too. Down under you there are gas pipes, water pipes, sewage pipes - and that dump of industrial waste and domestic refuse up the road. You're sick and tired and fed up and getting depressed.

One sure way to get help is to call in a dowser who knows his or her earth energy divining, who does not simply dowse for water. So you will more than likely require the services of a druid or druidess, who are about the only people who specialise in this field of healing the Earth - your Earth that your home is placed on.

One method is for the druid diviner to dowse the ley lines for you, draw up a map, show you the lines to get rid of - by driving an iron rod into the ground upstream of the negative energy, thus diverting it harmlessly away and grounding it so that it will do no harm to anybody. It is an efficient method of operation providing there is space around the surroundings of your house - or indeed your business premises if business is unexpectedly on the downturn!

The very best way is the use of The Spirals of Tranquillity. All 64 of the colours of the local Earth Star spectrum can be completely harmonised with no disruption at all by a druid who knows his business. Once the Earth Star on which your home stands is rebalanced you will be living in perfect harmony with your environment, even with all the modem muck, as described above, all around you. Your problem is that there are so few people, even in the bigger Druid Orders, trained sufficiently to carry out the necessary clearing operation.

The balance of the earth energies once comprised the energy cover around the world in a symmetrical flowing pattern of purity. If you wish to restore this balance to your house and garden, but can't find a druid or druidess qualified to do so in short order, while you are waiting there is something you can do yourself to restore a temporary balance. A simple and cheap way is to place quartz or rock crystal in a symmetrical pattern around your house and garden.

You should orient the gemstones North, South, East, West, following the pattern of the six-pointed "Star of David", with one placed in the centre. The sun, moon, planets and stars, acting through this Earth Star shape, will soon begin to change your whole environment, actually bring about an upturn in your fortunes by projecting and holding a vibrationary balance

Chapter Eight

The Psychic Fires of Ireland

THE WINDOW

At Newgrange the cairn-temple is carefully positioned over an underground water flow. Newgrange is a complex construction built precisely to incorporate and amplify earth energies. It was a power station of super energies sadly allowed to run down by those ignorant of how to recharge that huge battery. As the archaeologists rebuilt Newgrange they removed a block of quartz, as they noted in their daily work journal, from the window box. It had a 'partner' somewhere in the wreckage. These two blocks of quartz were the panes of the window box.

These two blocks of quartz in the window box over the door acted as polarising filters, splitting the white light of the sun. The exterior wall was covered with whitequartz in ancient times and the restoring archaeologists are to be congratulated in getting this right. For its purpose was to build up the massive earth energies between the quartz-faced wall and the kerbstones, creating a whirlpool of the most powerful energies to pulse through the quartz window panes, then down along the inner passageway to explode into the cruciform sacred chamber. Thereby were concentrated the most sacred energies on Earth as the priest impregnated the priestess and the child was conceived of the holy spirit, the divine child who would grow to rule at Tara.

All the energy thus captured was concentrated into the centre of the mound, which became a giant earth energies capacitor. This energy was carefully regulated and radiated outwards through the energy grids, from cairn to stone circle and on to standing stone all across the land in a huge countrywide grid.

Trees, vast forests, were important too. In those days the whole of Britain and Ireland consisted of mass afforestation to act as insulators and keep the energies in close to the land. Thus our reverence for trees! The journalists among you will now understand that we do not actually worship trees. We know how important they were for our survival across the aeons, acting as a blanket to keep the sacred earth energies from escaping off into space.

In Egypt the priesthood of the Pyramids were busy accomplishing the same task, just as the Mayans, Incas and Aztecs were in Central and South America. The Holy of Holies in the Temple of Jerusalem was built over a powerful underground water spiral, which made it extremely dangerous for the uninitiated to enter.

THE DOOR

Solstice is the Latin word for "sun standing still". At the times of the winter and summer solstices the sun seems to stand still.

On the night before the winter solstice the great
sealing stone was rolled across the doorway of Newgrange. The door was closed. Now the rays of the sun could activate the quartz crystal window and the sacred energies within.

THE TRIPLE SPIRAL

They engraved the triple spiral within the cairn temple of Newgrange, repeated it on standing stone K52 to the rear, engraving the constellation of Draco the dragon upon it to give those scientists among us who understand Precession, the date of their construction of Newgrange. On the right side of K52 stone they gave us a complete "computerised" printout of the triple energies involved.

IN THE EYE OF THE SUN

We hear the chants of the druids. We hear the voices from the circle. We listen to the heaven-inspired wisdom of the Archdruid as he stands on the capstone of a cromleach in the eye of the sun. Under the old oak tree we gaze upon the aged druid teaching young disciples the mystic lore in verses never to be written. We gaze upon the convocation of kings and chieftains at Tara, before whom the Wise discourse upon the Brehon Laws.

Then we see the druid as patriot, resisting the invader, intoning the Battle Hymn of the Gael. In wonder we wait upon the deliberations of these grand observers of sun and moon, planets and stars, reading the signs from the heavens and writing their books in stone across the land.

Over the past two hundred years druidry has been so blatantly claimed by

Episcopals that the Irish, the Scots, the Manx, the Cornish, and the Bretons would seem to have only minor places in that sacred inheritance. There are few Druidic stone remains in Wales. Ireland is richer than Wales in all but Roman ruins. It is a disgrace upon Ireland that her Druids should have been so long neglected and the honours of mystic wisdom be so appropriated.

Due to reverence of Rome the Irish have been less than enthusiastic about druidic ancestral pride and associated Gaelic glory. The Irish are learning that the power of our Gaelic spirituality needs no foreign component, because Ireland had its fabulous druids and traditional lore justifies the Irish people in the acknowledgement of those Magi who were more than human. The revival of all that is anciently Gaelic has given great prominence to druidic lore. That after fifteen centuries the organisation called The Order of Druids in Ireland has publicly proclaimed the creed of our forefathers has startled many.

Chapter Nine

The Theory and Practice of Druidry

I have discovered that over the centuries the ley lines have been bending westward, away from the mass industrial concentrations of mainland Europe and Britain. These ley fluctuations and reversals affect how the dates of the Druidic festivals are fixed.

I have come across a few books that I have found useful, although I did not find anything of a practical nature in the mythology, so replete and repetitive in so many 'druid' books, and so off-putting for the scientist or technologist who desires to become a druid. I know some of them and they may approach me in the knowledge that I am as hard-headed as they are when it comes to scientific proofs.

Since it is known that the ancient Druids purposely scrambled things to prevent the knowledge falling into the hands of those not equipped to use it, a lot of knowledge needs to be unscrambled before it can be understood and used properly. Puzzling it out keeps me busy. I'd much rather devote more time to it than having to administer the only Irish Druid Order at the same time.

People keep asking me what robes they should wear. In the climate of these islands thermal long johns under heavy outerwear, woolly headgear and warm footwear are more appropriate for latter day druids. There is no reason why cloaks and robes cannot be tidy, colourful and even decorated. But they do need to be warm.

Magic will work perfectly well if one is clad in a mac and wellies. After all, if it is such a potent force capable of working between one plane and another, across space and time, how could it possibly be impeded by a mere wisp of cotton, wool or polyester?

I suppose the yen to dress up in fine robes, even with the prospect of freezing one's bum off, is what has led to the evolution of the TV Witch resplendent in silk, sequins and embroidery. Such finery would not last long amid the bracken, branches and brambles of an oak or ash grove.

I have been told by an English Wiccan lady to throw my computer away. I replied that if my computer speeds up the work then it is a legitimate tool, whilst the enormous flashy sword of a TV witch is not. The telluric force of earth energy is, because of the increased gravity, much stronger at full and new moons; well, not so much 'stronger' as at the peak of its flow. Rain is known to occur shortly, about three days, after full and new moons. The actual full or new moon period is usually relatively calm and fine. The occurrence of rain correlates very closely with the moon cycle. Major conjunctions of planets cause weather disturbance and earthquakes. They never told you that about climate change! My coordination is a bit off at times when the East wind is blowing a lot of industrial pollution in here from Britain and Europe. I love when we get a good fresh Westerly gale to blow all the muck back where it belongs. If you're a 'sensitive' you'll probably feel like that too. The government should give away an electric car for every household, rather than keep on sending billions to the Paris Accord Swindle!

DRUIDIC SCIENCE OUTLAWED

The original belief system of most of Europe was druidic and it is a pity that druidry is not being used to unify Europe. We know that the ancient druids were immersed in the sciences, astronomy, mathematics and medicine in particular. Indeed they could be called the world's first cosmologists. When the early missionaries arrived one of the first things they did was to throw all that marvellous druidic science out the window. Being simple "hot gospellers" they did not understand it. Early Irish science was replaced by gospel parables, fables, tales, legends and above all by 'Celtic mythology' transformed in monasteries in a bid to create an 'Irish old testament' to fit in with the New Testament they brought with them. The druids, of course, cared less about fable, but they were the victims of it. Monkish mythology casts the recalcitrant druids as the 'bad guys' and the lesser Order of Fili who converted as the 'good guys', canonising several of the latter as Christian saints. With the proscription of Druidry, indeed its actual extermination, science was excommunicated and banished in early Christian Ireland. People, especially scientists, do not have to be reminded about Church persecution.

Gallileo's experiments, together with the works of two other 'heretics', the Danish astronomer Tycho Brahe and the German astronomer Johannes Kepler, paved the way for Newtonian physics. The English writer Thomas Digges postulated the possibility of a vast, even infinite, universe in 1576. He writes of "the orb of stars fixed infinitely up ...perpetually shining glorious lights innumerable far exceeding our Sun both in quantity and quality". One wonders what druid he had been talking to, or indeed if he were one himself.

Most unfortunate of all was the courageous Italian monk Giordano Bruno, who insisted that there were "innumerable suns and an infinite number of earths revolving around these suns". For his troubles he was burned at the stake.

Western cosmology began at least three and a half thousand years ago as they timed the moment of the Midwinter Solstice through their perfectly aligned window box of Newgrange, that ancient 'cathedral' and astronomical observatory in the Boyne Valley of Ireland. Cosmology is defined as the science of the universe.

Today experiment and theory enable us to look back to one millionth of a trillionth of a second after the Big Bang, to what we believe to be the origin of the universe fifteen thousand million years ago. Cosmology starts from that moment, continuing right throughout the evolution of the cosmos, which 'grew' from being the tiniest fraction of the size of a proton to an expanse towards infinity. Concerned Catholics will be assured to learn that Pope Pius XII accepted the Big Bang in 1951 so they have the Church's permission to believe in it! In fact the Belgian Catholic priest Georges Hemi Lemaitre developed the concept of the Big Bang in the years 1927 to 1933.

The Big Bang was just that - a giant explosion. However, the aftermath of the Big Bang did not (and still does not) move into existing space - it created and still creates space as it expands. The universe at the split second before creation existed under very different scientific laws.

As Stephen Hawking explains, the laws of science would not have applied before the Big Bang.

It was not until 1964, however, that Big Bang theory gained widespread scientific acceptance. That year two American radio astronomers discovered what appeared to be the dim afterglow of the Big Bang, an all-pervasive radiation with a temperature of less than three degrees above absolute zero. It is known as Cosmic Background Radiation and gives us an idea of what the universe was like a mere three hundred thousand years after creation.

If you look at the night sky through binoculars or a telescope you will see clusters of stars and galaxies. This is what you envisage when you think about the universe. It is what you do not see that is more important. If modern cosmologists are right - and there is every reason and logic to believe they are - the stars we see in the sky represent one percent of the matter of the universe. Most of the matter created by the Big Bang is completely alien to us, invisible to our eyes and beyond our senses and experience.

People hunger for knowledge of life, of death, of after-death, and of the Otherworld. Druidry seeks, finds and explains. Fifteen centuries ago we were almost there before we were so rudely interrupted. It is from this point that we eventually go beyond the Big Bang, beyond the triple spiral where all knowledge and wisdom flows.

THE FIFTH FORCE OF THE COSMOS.

Stephen Hawking was a druid but he didn't know it. There's nothing strange in this. Millions of people, the world over, are druids too. They don't know it either. I have read almost everything Stephen has written in his books.

I never met him. Yet I feel that I knew him very well. Stephen is recognised as one of the world's greatest living scientists. He was more closely identified with Black Hole theory than anybody else. At times Stephen said straight out that God does not exist. At other times he writes as if a belief in a concept of a creator is in his mind. In this he thought like certain modern druids. Certainly Stephen Hawking rejected the simplistic childlike picture of God as a sort of male or female entity in human terms, as a sort of superman or lovely goddess, or even a combination of both. The astronomers among our ancient druids regarded God as a kind of all-pervasive, all-powerful energy across time and space. Churches and religions did not enter Hawking's consciousness, or indeed his life. Like the intellectuals among the druids he regarded preaching of all such matters as perhaps morally useful at times but not for him. He believed, not in Otherworld, but in Other Worlds. Druids who felt the Otherworld would not go so far as Stephen in denial of Supernature. But I am sure Stephen Hawking would have allowed this druid to stand up on his frail shoulders and gaze across his universe.

Druidic science concurs with all the scientific disciplines of the present day, but with some differences, the most important being about the existence of the telluric force of earth energy. As Hawking and company are searching for the Theory of Everything, today's scientists just might consider that there is a fifth force in the universe. Several scientists today are looking into the realm of metaphysics (beyond known science), which was the supreme territory of our ancient ones. Occultists, including some druids, are so convinced of the superiority of 'Magick', Metaphysics, Parapsychology and the Paranormal that they reject orthodox science out of hand. This gets them nowhere. Let them pause for a moment and reflect.

Newton's laws of gravitation, published as his Principia in 1687, was found to be applicable to all motion in the solar system, so accurate that they were used to postulate the planet Neptune which could not even be seen by telescopes at the time, and also showed the orbits of Mars, Jupiter and Saturn to be accurate. Nearly three hundred years later the Americans used Newton's Principia when they programmed their rockets at Cape Kennedy for the successful moon landing in 1969. They didn't need to use Einsteinian calculations, more accurate than Newton's, as the difference is negligible around our solar system. Suffice it here to say that Relativity only comes into the picture in measurements very close to huge gravitational objects, such as our sun. 'Weightlessness' too in space is exactly computed by Newtonian gravitational laws - these facts should keep many a 'faery wiccan' foot on the ground, depending of course on Newtonian calculations.

I emphasise that druidic, occult, esoteric, metaphysical and related studies of this New Enlightenment must all be firmly grounded in the laws of theoretical physics, although everybody is entitled to his or her reasonable flights of fancy which might even turn up an original idea - even a breakthrough now and then in a millennium. I am convinced that cosmologists like Hawking was, are on the right track, their only drawback being that they are still a bit too conservative.

Risk of personal ridicule is a small price to pay for moving the boundaries of science out to be more all-encompassing. Einstein's relativity began with his constant worrying about the nature of gravity. Maybe it was not a force at all, he considered. Gravity might be due to certain properties of the medium it is operating in, that is, space itself, he mused. He did not realise it but he was staring at the telluric force inherent in all bodies in space.

Einstein decided that space is not flat but curved. His set of mathematical equations described the curvature of space and the distribution of mass in the universe. This is important for you to grasp so that you will easily understand relativity:

Einstein held that matter tells space how to curve and then space tells matter how to move - not simple, but a new way to describe gravitation. A mind flip is necessary to jump between two pictures of gravitation, Einstein and Newton's.

I postulate the telluric force, inherent in all bodies, in all matter throughout the universe, as the force responsible for actually curving space, within Einstein's theory. I learned all this in the Physics department of Trinity College Dublin when I should have been breadboarding electronics exercises in computer science!

Therefore bodies moving through curved space do not travel in straight lines but along the paths of curved space. These paths are known as geodesics Now, wouldn't it be interesting if NASA tested this. The telluric force extends not only through and around a body such as the Earth, but out into space, through and around all bodies in space, from one body to the next.

Mathematically Einstein's relativity stands up - but it still doesn't completely describe the stuff of gravity, the force between bodies in space that causes them to attract rather than to repel. The greatest discoveries in science have come from those who have and know how to use innate , almost mystical, abilities that are inherent in many of us, but have been lost since dogma took control over the human brain, mind or psyche, unnaturally swamping our higher powers or spirit/souls. The ancient druids knew, as many of us do today, how to develop and use these higher powers. Our ancient Druids are documented to withdraw and live in the depths of the forests just as talented monks did much the same throughout the following centuries in cloistered calm. The hermit wisely refuses to give up his solitude for anybody or anything - love, fame or money.

Albert Einstein was no more of a mathematician than Stephen Hawking. They both picked up the mathematics they needed as they delved more into cosmology and the secrets of the universe. Einstein referred to the idea that got him going as "the happiest thought of my life". While sitting bored at his desk in Berne in Switzerland one day in 1907: "A certain thought occurred to me - if a person falls freely he will not feel his own weight! I was startled and this simple thought made a deep impression on me. It impelled me towards a theory of gravitation. It was the happiest moment of my life." Although Jewish by descent Einstein rejected the biblical idea of God. His activities and ideas came under attack. An anti-Einstein organisation was set up. A man who was convicted of inciting others to murder Einstein was fined a mere six dollars on conviction. When a book was published, "One Hundred Authors against Einstein" he replied: "If I were wrong, one would have been enough!"

On proving relativity Einstein wrote to his close friend, the Dutch physicist Paul Ehrenfest:

"I was beside myself with ecstasy for days. Imagine my joy that the new law of curvature obeys the principle of relativity ... the years of searching in the dark for a truth that one feels but cannot express - the intense desire and the alterations of confidence and misgiving until one breaks through to clarity and understanding - are only known to him who has experienced them himself."

Einstein never doubted that he had been privileged to glimpse into the very mathematical mind and physical heart of all things. James R. Newman spoke of Einstein's 30-page paper " on the Electrodynamics of Moving Bodies" as embodying a vision. He observed that poets and prophets are not the only ones to have visions, but that scientists experience them as well. They glimpse a peak perhaps never again seen, but their landscape is forever changed. Their lives are spent elaborating on the vision that others might follow. Those ancient Watchers of the Skies, the druid astronomers, had such visions too. We still do.

THE MAGIC OF THE CRAFT

Millions of people throughout the world are becoming increasingly disenchanted with the established religions and churches and are turning towards a broad spectrum of beliefs and practices found under the rainbow of the New Age. Many adherents of the New Age, although not belonging to any Order or Grove, increasingly acknowledge the leading role of the druids. Paradoxically, many Irish druids would regard themselves as Old Age.

The Hermetic Order of the Golden Dawn, boasting Yeats, Maud Gonne and Bram Stoker among its Irish members, was the single most important influence that transformed modern Druidry at the end of the 19th and the beginning of the 20th century. The Order taught that personal transformation was closely linked to world transformation and that with the dawning of the New Age human evolution would take a huge leap forward. To join the Order applicants were administered the following oath:

"I solemnly promise and swear that with the Divine permission I will from this day forward apply myself to the Great Work which is so to purify and exalt my spiritual nature that with the Divine aid I may at length attain to be more than human, and thus gradually raise and unite myself to my Magus and Divine Genius, and that in this event I shall not abuse the great power entrusted to me ."

"To Know, to Will, to Dare, to Keep Silent" is the Occult obligation still in force in Druid Orders, although "to Keep Silent" has long fallen by the wayside as Druid Orders publicly perform our ceremonial "on the heel of the stone and in the eye of the sun." A word of warning here from Yeats himself, which applies not only to druids but to all who practice the high magic art. He advises that anybody who has not achieved the fifth or sixth adept grades (equivalent today to Druid of Ireland) should never attempt a magical operation.

These were very high Golden Dawn adept grades. Druids, like writers, artists, poets, musicians etc (which many of us are) are sensitives and all such people will benefit from this advice.

As a person evolves through the practice of Druidry his or her vibrations change, their physical bodies become less gross, finer, until at the peak of evolution can become as delicate as gossamer. This process speeds up your evolution several thousand years ahead of those around you and you will find yourself getting less interested in ordinary everyday affairs like gossiping with the neighbours or going to pubs, cinemas and racetracks. You will also find it much easier to do such things as give up alcoholic drink, cigarettes, diet and exercise properly. The practice of druidry will contribute to your good health and longevity.

In an isolated castle in Ireland the Druid Yeats planned to establish the Celtic Order of Mysteries which would employ occult means to achieve Irish Unity and Independence. In many ways we are still awaiting the realisation of the dream. Yet the druid may smile, for we are almost there.

Many years ago I grasped what Colin Wilson meant by what he calls our "Faculty X" in his bestselling book The Occult. I can switch it on at will ever since. It's probably the Irish Druid blood in me. The short pendulum whirls around like a helicopter propeller in my hand so much so that I have (keep my hand stretched perfectly flat to stop it knocking off my outstretched fingers. Similarly I get pins-and-needles in my hands and feet and the "head-in-the-bucket" effect as I approach ancient sites.

On a dull day I can switch on "Faculty X" and a grey street takes on a golden aura. Druidry is totally misrepresented in the schools' history curricula of Ireland in a surprising self-rejection of their golden heritage by those who consider themselves intelligent creatures, intelligent enough to determine the curricula. By their choices let them be judged.

Because of the Precession of the Equinoxes, an astronomical occurrence that need not worry you at this stage, the point where the sun passes from south to north of the celestial equator at the vernal equinox, is now passing into the sign of Aquarius. Planetary conjunctions such as that of the midwinter solstice of 1995 have been taken into consideration in determining that we arrived in the spiritual Age of Aquarius on that significant date. Aquarius is a fixed air sign, air bearing water which signifies the astral, travel into Otherworld and across the universe.

It has been alleged that the New Age has much in common with Eastern religions, but this is only a small part of the unfolding scenario. Druidry, swift becoming the New Age philosophy, has its traditions firmly grounded in Ireland and the West. Gurus from the East have come and gone with the pop stars of the Sixties. A quarter of the population of the U.S.A now believe in reincarnation. Many now believe in the cyclical nature of life, continuing revelation from beings beyond, the identity of man with God, the need for meditation, visualisation and other consciousness-changing techniques, occult practices such as astrology, tarot, pendulum divination, the second sight, the third eye, scrying, telepathy, dream interpretation, telepathy, telekinesis, psychokinesis, ESP, apports, spiritual healing, herbalism and alternative medicine, prophecy, poetic invocation and communication with the Otherworld, paraphysics and parapsychology, hypnotherapy and neuro linguistic programming. All these are represented in modern Druidry.

Our ancient Druids had no need of any stranger to come to the Land of Erin to give them any philosophy, for the triple spiral etched into the womb of Newgrange, drawings of far-off galaxies that cannot be seen with the naked eye, shows that they knew of the divine philosophy above and beyond all things. And they could only have evolved as the aeons went by into pure spirit, spirit that is still in the land, in the mounds, in the stones and the starry skies above. They are still here. You will find them in yourself, for they are in your very genes.

"Trips into Other Realms" can be experienced under guidance at the "psycho-centres" mushrooming in big cities across the world. I think one would more readily experience a real trip into Otherworld sitting atop a faery mound, a rath, out in the wilderness of rural Ireland. Try the mound of Dowth, near Newgrange, and you should see what I mean.

CREATION

Being a brilliant cosmologist, Hawking was using his head all the time he sat in his wheelchair. Just as the ancient Druids used to do when they wanted to know.

They slept all day every day and stayed in their darkened quarters all night every night. We have it in the mythology that on one occasion they thus pondered a single question for fifty-three days and nights until finally they came out into the glaring light of day - inspired with the answer.

Now let us go back in our minds to the Big Bang and to exactly what the Creator did at that point in time and space. At the Big bang God divided himself off. God was the tiny atom that exploded, or as the Druids signified, the cosmic egg. And the spark of God is within every one of us from that split second when God divided himself off, providing part of his energy to cause and direct the Big Bang and part of himself to furnish the subatomic first particle. So the existence of God as a separate entity is true. But the existence of God within every one of us, within all creation, is also true, and that part within us remains connected to that part of God that remained and remains outside of space and time as we know it.

Why? This was Stephen Hawking, the scientist, trying to get to grips with philosophy and theology which he honestly admitted were not within his discipline - why did God do it? We can get rid of this 'why'. We can give so many different answers and any one of them can be true. You just choose your own 'why'. Or if you are a practising member of a church they usually choose it for you under the heading of doctrine. You choose your own Why which is valid for you. My own 'why' - I think God keeps splitting off little micro atoms from himself to create all sorts of universes throughout all time, that the Big Bang he caused to create this universe of ours may or may not have been the first universe he created, and that he may still be creating as I write.

" At the Big Bang and other singularities, all the laws would have broken down, so God would still have had complete freedom to choose what happened and how the universe began." - Stephen Hawking, A Brief History of Time.

THE FILE-FAITH

The File-Faith (pronounced Filleh-Faw") was another name druids used when the word "Druid" itself was outlawed in early Christian Ireland. As you can see the title consisted of running the two grades of File and Faith together. This has come down through the generations in the language of the Irish tradition so that there are parts of Ireland today where the Druid is mentioned as the "File Faith". It seems that Druids have survived right into the present in Ireland under this title.

THE WAY OF THE WEST

The Druids were the ruling members of an autocratic priestly caste. Quite apart from their reputed magical powers, they wielded considerable political and cultural influence among their people, the effect of which has sifted down through our western inner tradition and is part of everybody's spiritual inheritance today and into the future. What they undoubtedly did was to systemize a great deal of that tradition, giving it structure and sophistication.

Though the druids insisted on the transmission of the Hidden Tradition by oral means only, they were anything but illiterate. Their "mouth-to-ear" method of imparting spiritual instruction was a time-honoured system of "passing the Word" directly along a carefully chosen line of consciousness connecting successive generations of certain families and clans. A tradition received in this way through direct human contacts linking inner intelligences is far more alive than if handed down on paper. What the druids put forward was their own synthesis of the principles, that is, they selected specific keys and leading points from the more ancient creeds and codes and then interpreted them in a more practical way for the needs of the people of these islands. This is their main contribution to our Way of the West. It has left indelible marks on the shape of our philosophic and moral codes.

The druids had superb command of one art in particular, that of oration. It was a thrilling experience to partake of a druid "Preach-In". The dullest minds began to open and unused intelligences awakened to instructions and information hitherto unavailable. The druids taught in terse simple terms with allegorical allusions and local phraseology. People listened in fascination and awe to these amazing men who moved multitudes with their tongues and gestures in their sermons from the mounds. The western tradition is indebted to them for an impact of inner awakenings at a time when we really needed rousing from a torpid state of spiritual slumber. The druids held to a "chosen people" or "sanctification of the elect" teaching. Only those souls who came up to pre-specified spiritual standards would make the grade in the afterlife. There was little hope for the rest.

What the druids did for the West was lay the foundation stones of alternative inner ways which later developed into Catholicism and Protestantism.

Christians trace back to the old martyred sacred king concept that prevailed before the Druids, and that was afterwards acted out by Christ. The major difference between Druid and Catholic is one of the relationship of Man with God. Catholics believe in the principle of sacrifice affecting salvation - the druids believed, and still do, in direct individual applications to Divinity which might or might not find favour.

Hard on the druids' heels advanced Roman Imperialism with its multi-religious military might. Centuries before this, the European Celts, urged on by the druids, had smashed their way into the young city of Rome, a history lesson never forgotten by the Romans. Looked upon therefore as a highly dangerous counterforce to the new Roman Empire, the druids were virtually exterminated. Druids were leading the resistance movement in the Celtic countries so they and their families and clans were smashed forever by Rome. The druids survived for a few centuries more in Ireland until they too had to disappear for the sake of political expediency in a Europe of Holy Roman emperors and kings.

To break up an outer organisation with political and military power is a calculable operation. To eradicate the inner effects such an organisation may have made on the minds and souls of a people is a different affair entirely. Druids may have died in large numbers, but they stayed alive within the

western tradition.
Moreover, many of them, as "File-Faith" for instance, simply faded into a camouflaged obscurity, continued as an underground movement, and waited for another day.

THE FAR SIDE OF THE SUN

The authors of such books as The Tomb of God may or may not have proved the burial place of Jesus to be somewhere under Mount Cardou near Rennes le Chateau in the Languedoc province of France - but they have dug the tomb of Rome. Dr. Barbara Thiering, that remarkable lay theologian who wrote Jesus the Man, leaves Jesus as a seventy-year-old man in Rome. There are authors who compellingly write that he was buried in Kashmir, or that the Knights Templar unearthed his bones under the Temple of Jerusalem. Genuine Christians are in despair. I can understand how many of them are in tears. Their whole world is centred on Jesus as the resurrected Son of God and this is coming under increasing academic and professional scrutiny.

Despite the overwhelming evidence, people should not despair. For it is the real life and death of Jesus that is being discovered, not the tomb of God. It is for the disappointed now to turn to God in a hopeful and meaningful way, in a spiritually grounded belief that we are all the children of God, that there is an Otherworld as the druids proved and constantly held through persecution and genocide. Their wisdom, their teachings, are now more urgent to a wondering world than ever: As we stand in front of the Tomb of Rome, over it stands the Druid. For truly he saw it in the heavens and wrote it upon the Earth. Sixteen centuries ago the missionaries landed on our shores, without the memory and without the understanding, to convert the "Heathen Irish" to the legends of Rome.

And the Ancient Ones left. Nobody knows where. Perhaps to the far side of the Sun.

Chapter Ten

Manipulating the Force...

The sun's brilliant low glare between the standing stones embodies the relationship between the seasons of the sun, the circles of the stones and the watchers of the skies. Across north western Europe there are over a thousand arrangements of these stones, ranging from single stones to complex circles to the magnificent edifices of astronomical observation such as Newgrange and Stonehenge. We now know that Newgrange, Stonehenge and the rest were forms of astronomical computers, that they amplified and manipulated the earth energies, that they were centres of mystical and mysterious workings, centres of Druidcraft.

ATLANTEAN DRUIDS

The building of Stonehenge began as far back as 2,900 BC. The Boyne Valley megaliths started in 4,500 BC. These megalithic structures predate the great pyramid of Giza, which was built around 2,720 BC. Dr. Richard Kearney, in the introduction to his classic The Irish Mind, writes that Ireland was inhabited as far back as 10,000 BC.

There is now no doubt that a learned race came into the Boyne Valley around 4,500 BC. What manner of people were these? It is highly unsatisfactory to dub them "the Boyne Valley people" and leave them at that. It is clear that they were highly intelligent and advanced and knew a lot more than primitive 'priests' or tribal shamans.

This period is left "on hold" because few are prepared to admit that the presence of this highly evolved race in the Boyne Valley circa 4,500 BC is an outstanding mystery of our planet, if not the outstanding mystery! Ireland cannot continue to build its house of megalithic archaeology on sand. Slowly, through the minutes, the hours, the days, the months, the years, it is coming to me in bits and pieces. Sometimes things occur to me and I painstakingly try to unravel it all. Of course the ancient structures were built by proto-druids, those I prefer to describe as Atlantean druids, a more telling description, if for no other reason than that they lived on the edge of the Atlantic and we still do.

My friend Rollo Maughfling, Archdruid of England, Titular Druid of Avondale and Wicklow.

On the 6th day of the moon the Druids cut the mistletoe, Julius Caesar wrote

The Order of Druids in Ireland, of which the author is Chosen Chief.

The Celtic Order of Mysteries was to be established by WB Yeats in this quaint castle on Lough Key, but the mystic poet abandoned the project after Maud Gonne left him.

Archdruid McGrath pictured in blue-green robe on the right of this druid group on Tara, October 2006

SECRET OF THE SITES

The stone circle of Callanish in the Outer Hebrides clearly demonstrates the celestial surveying skills of our ancestors. The Merry Maidens stone circle at the other extreme of the Land of Britain consists of nineteen granite stone blocks near the sea at Land's End in Druidic Cornwall. There are at least eight star alignments among the Maidens, including alignments to Antares, Capella and Arcturus. druids are now employing equipment like geiger counters, magnetometers, ultrasound detectors, scintillation counters, electro-magnetic field detectors, infrared cameras, and our own computer programmes to manipulate findings. We have the qualified personnel too: because now you will find druids in all the professions and in every career. Therefore we can no longer be dismissed as amateurs or cranks. No druid has ever dismissed the opinions of another human being because of his or her differing beliefs or religion.

The results of our researches are startling, not to druids as we expected as much, but to those members of the general public who have been lucky enough to get to read about them so far. At the druidic 'tombs' in Baltinglass in County Wicklow, radio signals emanate from the monuments! Newgrange, on the other hand, as well as one of the cairns at Loughcrew, blank out radio transmissions - they are both on the same major leyline across Ireland.

The earliest discoveries by the British earth energy societies show that ultrasound detectors operating in the 25 - 80 kilohertz frequency band (25 - 80 thousand cycles per second) have detected certain stones which emit an ultrasonic click at sunrise and sunset, with a varying ultrasonic pulse detected intermittently at several other sites.
The sites investigated have produced even more exciting results. Scientists have long acknowledged that our environment is a whole complex of radiation, composed of energies from beyond the Earth, mostly of solar origin. Scientists also recognise electro-magnetic forces associated with the Earth, also Earth radioactive decay, and all the various electromagnetic forces associated with human activity such as radio and television broadcasting including MMDS TV radiation, mobile phone radiation, continuous radar pulsation, and your 'ordinary' electricity supply. This energy soup of everyday living, a lethal mix giving rise to cancers, tumours and Alzeimer's disease, is collectively known as background radiation. Some sites give higher than background readings while others, notably in rural Ireland,

Cornwall and the Scottish Highlands, give lower readings. This goes a long way towards proving that the stone circles act as shields against radiation - and that they will, when finally overpowered by a mix of radiation and pollution, soak in that lethal mix like sponges, safeguarding the people, animals and land around. They were programmed to do this - thousands of years ago

Measurements taken as far back as 1985 prove that Geiger counter readings were actually halved by the shields. In 1982 a steady drop in radiation was detected as a thunderstorm approached an ancient site - the exact opposite to what should happen. Again we see the site acting as a protective shield for the local population.

Almost all of the megalithic sites investigated display dowsing or divining effects. As already explained the stone circles are aligned to underground water and earth energy easily discovered by the divining twig, dowsing rods and the pendulum. As few can personally afford all that expensive electronic equipment, dowsing requires little outlay. And virtually anybody can dowse. Some can do it best with the traditional hazel twig. More can do it with rods which are simply cut from a wire coat hanger.

Most people find the short pendulum easiest - in fact most women start off by using their necklaces! You can graduate from this to using the long pendulum, which you should make out of an old fishing rod - before I claim patent rights! You can practice dowsing anywhere, even in the privacy of your own home, as some people do.

Chapter Eleven

Spellcraft - the Ritual of Cursing

THE GLAN DICENN

The Fili of ancient Ireland used the ritual known as the Glam Dicenn. It is a survival of druidic custom. A ninth century Gaelic work refers to it under the heading Corrguineacht and describes it as consisting of "being on one foot and with one hand and one eye making the Glam Dicenn ". From this it appears that while uttering the verse or verses the poet stood on one foot, raised one arm and closed one eye. There are some exaggerated conditions attached to the Glam Dicenn later on by the Church, but the following style of ritual would have been followed:

The poet commenced with a fasting. He went up on the summit of a hill. He faced in the direction of the residence of he whom he wished to utter the Glam Dicenn against, with the north wind blowing at the time of the spell. This form of satire in ancient times seems to have been a most serious and formal manner of effectively cursing someone.

In fact the word 'curse' comes from the Irish language. It derives from the word cursachadh, which meant 'abuse' in ninth century Gaelic. It has since fallen into disuse in Irish but has found a permanence in English.
There are several words connected with cursing in Irish Gaelic. Mallacht comes from the same source as malediction. Escaine is ancient Irish that describes the idea of making unclean. Other Irish words associated with ritual cursing are conntracht meaning contrary or against, and strangely, the Irish word to pray, guiodoireacht. There is an ancient belief in Ireland that a curse develops a life of its own once pronounced. Colonel Wood Martin in his book, Traces of the Elder Faiths in Ireland, Volume 11, notes that "a curse must fall on something; if it does not fall on the person on whom it is invoked, it will remain for seven years in the air, ready to fall on the head of the individual who pronounced the malediction." In Gaelic there is a saying that expresses this: Faoi bhun crainn a thiteas an duilluir -"under a tree falls its foliage!"

In the past the most helpless adult person was the widow. She usually had nothing. All she had left was her curse, and a widow's curse was one of the most feared things in the land. People were terrified of a Druid's curse, although such curses are so few that they are virtually unknown, and with the advent of the new religion they came to fear a priest's curse much more because the priests made full and frequent use of potent cursing.

If a person knows you cursed him and he is an adept he can send your curse back at you to strike you three times harder under the ancient Threefold Law of Return. It may also be the case that the person you curse is under protection from the Otherworld - if this is the case you are doomed! Peter Berresford Ellis mentions the hereditary curse on a section of his family and shows that he takes it very seriously indeed. As the description suggests, the hereditary curse fell on a person and his descendants.

The vicious injustice of this practice needs no comment from the fair-minded. The most famous hereditary curse in Ireland was on the family of the Marquis of Waterford. This family, named Beresford, took over the land and rank of the last Lord Power of Curraghmore after the Williamite War and, although the first Beresford married one of the dispossessed Powers, the older Irish families have always viewed the Beresfords with distaste. One of the Beresfords hanged a widow's only son in Seskin near Carrick-on-Suir for a trivial reason and the mother cursed him and his descendants for seven generations. All the owners of the Beresford lands have died violent deaths. This can be verified historically.

Although not the result of a curse, but perhaps as a result of some form of retribution, the author R.J. Stewart writes of the magical disappearance of the Reverend Robert Kirk of Aberfoyle (1644-?), the first translator of the Bible into Scots Gaelic, collector of early examples of faery lore and possessor of the Second Sight. There are accounts of certain persons who made trips to the Otherworld while still in bodily form. Some of these returned as seers or seeresses, while others like Robert Kirk remain lost but not dead. People were still trying to rescue Kirk from faeryland a generation ago as a result of local tradition that had continued on for 300 years.

Cursing was often accompanied by certain rituals, not all of them coming from the ancient past. Cursing from a height is more effective, so we have the saying, "he cursed her from a height" still in everyday speech. Some of the more interesting cursing ceremonies make use of stones called 'cursing stones'. This practice probably comes from a time when miniatures of standing stones and stone circles were used. A West Clare farmer in the last century was prosecuted for beating a beggar-woman. In his defence in court the man explained that she had threatened to "turn the stone of

Kilmoon against him". The Kilmoon stone was turned anti-clockwise by the curser while the words of doom were recited. The Kilmoon stone could turn one's mouth awry and make one look like a permanently deranged lunatic.

The famous Celtic scholar John O'Donovan speaks of another cursing stone he saw on Caher Island seven miles north of Renvyle Point in Galway. There is an ancient monastic site with some ruins on this island. The cursing stone was on the altar of the ruined church. If anybody felt wronged he went to the island, fasted and prayed. He turned the stone anti-clockwise as he cursed the wrongdoer. Then, if he was in the right, a storm arose and the cursed person was destroyed.

THE CURSE OF TARA CHALLENGED

The main earth energy line running through Tara enters Ireland at the Hill of Howth, the Beann Eadair of Druidic settlement fame which housed an ancient college and observatory, in north Dublin. It surges on via Loughcrew, the Carrowmore cromleach area, the great cairn atop Knocknarea hill in County Sligo and out into the Atlantic.

Not to muddle things with too much megalithic 'technology', St. Ruadhan ritually cursed Tara in the fifth century. He did this in revenge against the High King Diarmuid who had executed Ruadhan's cousin for disobeying orders. The quarrel had absolutely nothing to do with the druids, who were on the run for their very lives by this time. But Ruadhan obviously knew the druidic workings. He had a stone driven into the earth. Today this stone is still there, protruding five feet out of the ground in the old church graveyard at the entrance to Tara. This cursing stone splits off the inflowing ley line coming up from the well area, dividing the natural energy off and around the hill.

Duchas, Ireland's heritage service, has always refused to remove this cursing stone from the site as they feel it to be a national treasure! If they only knew the horror, sickness, violence and disaster this ugly stone has caused over the past fifteen centuries, not only to Tara but to the whole of Ireland , they would remove it and store it away. Such is the malignance of that stone that if you were to cast it into the depths of the sea it would still continue its evil ways by sinking ships! The best way to destroy it, of course, is to burn it on the site and thus crack it, as the Bretons have done to such stones.

At the start of 1997 with our Spring Equinox ceremony coming up I felt that something must be done. The cursing stone had in several ways ruined our Midsummer Solstice celebrations on Tara in the previous years since our return in 1993. I turned up at Tara on the morning of that Vernal Equinox at 10.00a.m. It was a working-day Thursday so only forty members were there out in the wilds. I went immediately to the offending stone. I 'tuned' in.

Straightaway I felt the familiar pain on the right side of my brain, confirming that there was going to be resistance by the force, by the shade of Ruadhan who had foolishly kept himself earthbound through all of fifteen centuries, such was his vengeful nature. By his wicked working of fifteen centuries before he had condemned his spirit to remain there as guardian of that cursing stone. I introduced myself aloud in Irish, stated who I was, and told Ruadhan that I would be back in an hour to start a magical operation to remove him. I then turned, walked away, and slowly drank a bottle of distilled water in the nearby Maguire's restaurant.

Everybody was excited there as I planned what I had to do. I had never removed the power of a cursing stone before - and this was probably the most powerful one in the world. If I could neutralise it for a few months until after Midsummer I would be more than happy.

I constructed a druidic circle. The circle, for as long as it would last, cut off all power to Ruadhan. Now all I had to do was persuade Ruadhan to leave, to overcome his stubborn spirit. I warned him. My assistants in turn warned me that the earth, on a cold spring morning, was warming up! A smaller 'linked' stone a couple of yards away was red hot! At that I did the very best thing a Druid could possibly do with Ruadhan - I lost my temper! I took off my Druid cloak and hurled it over the stone. Simultaneously I called on the God of the Druids to expel Ruadhan to the infernal regions. That did it - he was gone in a flash!

I asked my chief assistant, Archdruid John Murray of Kildare, now over in Vermont in the U.S.A., to hand me a small piece of triangular white quartz, which I consecrated, and pinned in under the stone to seal the ceremony. That should take care of Ruadhan, I thought, for a year and a day, according to ancient practice.

The consecrated quartz maintains a defensive shield of ten feet in diameter. The effectiveness of Tara as a powerhouse of magical energy was now restored for the time being. That year the Celtic tiger economy of Ireland simply soared. Ruadhan was gone for a couple of years. Since he returned the country is back in decline with a mushrooming national debt, but I believe that's an ancient Druidic revenge on the government that raped Tara with the M3 motorway. And now the Coronavirus plague.

Temporary measures are no use. The cursing stone of Tara will have to be removed or blasted , done simply by cracking it with fire.   Then with Ruadhan neutralised the country should prosper again.

Nobody should touch that stone as it can cause all kinds of illnesses, maladies, diseases, malignancies and cancers. People living around are in particular danger but so is everybody within a radius of seven miles from the Hill of Tara. After we neutralised Ruadhan we had marvellous results and great times on Tara. The mound beside the central mound, Cormac's House, is built over a negative water spiral some fifteen feet below.
The positive energy at the centre point of the central mound creates a massive lift-off point for the priesthood, when Ruadhan is not around!

High King Diarmuid died in battle in 558 AD. He was the last king to live on Tara.

The story began when King Diarmuid sent his messenger to a nobleman called Aed Guaire (Hugh Gorey) in the territory of Clare-Galway on the river Shannon. Diarmuid had made a law that all the doorways of his chieftains throughout Ireland were to be wider, the width of a spear, but Aed had not bothered to widen his own door. The king's agent arrived at Ead's door in his absence and insisted that he be admitted holding his spear horizontally. The doorway was widened and then the royal messenger entered. Aed turned up, saw his doorway destroyed, thought the king's messenger had done it and slew him. The king arrived and executed Aed, Ruadhan' s cousin, for the murder of his servant.

Now Ruadhan went into action. The saint was renowned for his love of cursing. Ruadhan took his friend, Brendan of Birr, with him and appeared before Diarmuid's palace on the hill of Tara. First the two monks rang their bells against the king and then fasted against him. This did not worry the tough king who in turn started to fast and pray against the two monks. They then realised that they were dealing with a formidable foe in their own field, so they decided to trick the king into breaking his fast. They pretended to eat, and when the king saw this from afar he decided to eat as long as they did. When he found out they had tricked him he began to curse Ruadhan and the saint replied in kind:

Diarmuid: "For what you've done Ruadhan you'll be rejected by the Blessed Trinity, because your monastery will be the first to decline in Ireland."

Ruadhan: "Your kingdom will decline first and none of your descendants will ever reign!"

Diarmuid: "Your beloved monastery will be deserted ..."

Ruadhain: "Your royal city will be empty within a hundred years."

In the ritual the actions of the monks with the ringing of bells, fasting and prayer seem very like a form of excommunication, which is of course the supreme cursing ritual of the Catholic Church.

Diarmuid never saw the two monks place the cursing stone in the ground at Tara that moonless night and cover it with clumps of bushes. The dereliction of Tara was then followed by the misery of the rest of Ireland, to this very day.

PRIEST CURSES THE CLAN McGRATH

Sleady castle near Modeligo in west Waterford is the ancestral home of my clan of the McGrath. It was built in the early seventeenth century. Members of the MacGrath family settled in the hilly area of Toumaneena between Dungarvan and Clonmel. They exercised great influence among the people. These McGraths became known as the Clanna Bui(The Yellow Clan). The Clanna Bui operated as Tithe proctors for the Church of Ireland and were influential with the authorities. They were able to operate on behalf of the Protestant Church on account of still being half-druids themselves who owed nothing but enmity to Rome.

The Clanna Bui were not very friendly with the Roman Catholic clergy, to put it mildly, until one member of the family became a priest at the beginning of the nineteenth century - then the situation changed radically.

Somewhere in the middle of the eighteenth century two men of the family had a huge disagreement on a business matter and they met in the village of Touraneena to discuss it. The two locked themselves in a room in the house, which can still be seen, and went from heated debate to ferocious argument and then to no-holds- barred fighting. So fierce was the fight that one killed the other. The authorities didn't do anything as nobody was sure whether it was a case of accidental death or not: there had been no witnesses in the locked room. So the survivor was not put on trial for his life. There were whispers going around, as there are to this very day, that the McGraths used their influence with the authorities to have the whole affair hushed up, but nobody will ever know.

What we do know is that on the Sunday following the killing the parish priest, a man by the name of Father Patrick Power, condemned McGrath publicly from the altar in Touraneena and finished his fire and brimstone from the pulpit by thoroughly cursing MacGrath with a slua-mhallacht, a general and comprehensive curse. This ferocious curse seems neither to have frightened nor tamed McGrath.

He never went to the Catholic Church. However on the Sunday following the curse he arrived in the little church in Touraneena, strode up to the altar and began to beat the priest. This incident was viewed as a sacrilege so the bishop decided to investigate the matter. The result was that the bishop decided in favour of McGrath and against the curses of Father Power. To punish the priest for the curse the bishop decreed that each Sunday henceforth he should go the long distance to Dungarvan to say mass in the morning and then come back to do the same in Touraneena.

Eventually one Sunday Father Power was delayed by wind and rain and he arrived after midday back in Toumaneena from Dungarvan. According to the strict contemporary regulations he dared not say mass at this time. He went to the church, where his congregation had waited patiently for an hour, and swore in a blind rage:

"As to those who are guilty of all this, the world will see that they won't have a day's luck and will disappear like the froth of the river."

McGrath died within a week of this final malediction. Local tradition has it that when his remains were being carried across the field to Knockboy burial ground (Cnoc Bui: "The Hill of the Clanna Bui"), Father Power who had cursed him saw someone replacing a gap-closing that had been opened to allow the funeral through:

"Leave it open", cried the distraught wild-eyed priest, "Leave it open! There are more of them to come!"

Within a year all the males of that generation of the Clanna Bui died and were brought to Knockboy. It seems that I share with fellow Druid Peter Beresford Ellis a cursed family background in County Waterford. Throughout the past two centuries there have been many unexplained deaths among the relatively young men of the McGraths of West Waterford.

Druidlore

Chapter Twelve

The Nature of the Druids

Nora Chadwick, author of The Celts, has pointed out that "the druids are the most advanced of all intellectual classes among the peoples of ancient Europe beyond the Greek and Roman world." In the second edition of his book, A Brief History of the Druids, Peter Berresford Ellis comes up with a new and exciting explanation of the word Druid. He derives the Irish root Dru to mean 'an immersion'.

He goes on to develop this so that the word Druid means a person who is "immersed in knowledge". I hastily accept this while the compliments are flying! And I am happy that no less person than Professor Daithi O'hOgain of the Department of Folklore at University College Dublin describes the linking of the word Druid with oak as somewhat fanciful:

The favourite tree of the (Irish) Druids was clearly the Rowan, and it was on wattles of this tree that Irish practitioners slept to have prophetic visions. The hazel tree was also important as evidenced by the Druid 's name Mac-Cuill (son of hazel) and also by lore concerning nine hazel trees at the source of the river Boyne, the nuts of which had a nucleus of wisdom.

All this follows from that grand old wizard of Irish druidic studies, Dr. Julius Pokorney of Vienna, who argued a century ago that the oak was not the prime tree of the Irish druids, although it does have its place alongside the rowan, the yew and the hazel. His contention that the druids originated in Ireland is of huge importance. Sir John Rhys in Celtic Folklore (1901) supports him.

Druidry was born in Ireland out of the advanced Boyne culture of beyond 3,500 BC, spreading very early across to Britain, across the channel to ancient Gaul, rooting among the Celtic nations from Galicia in Spain to Galatia in Asia Minor where the Celts built the great city of Ancyra (today's Ankara).

This fits in with the contention of Dr. Anne Ross and others that the ancient Germans and Danes practised forms of druidry. Berresford Ellis is correct in asserting that druidry stretched into Cisalpine Gaul, that is, Northern Italy. Domhnaill Gruamach insists that the ancient Etruscans of Italy practised druidry as well.

The importance of the oak must have come when druidry spread out from Ireland. I conclude that most of ancient Europe practised various forms of it. Druidry is the only religion that Ireland has ever given to the world although for the past fifteen centuries our missionaries have been the most energetic of all in preaching another.

Professor Fell maintains that our ancient Celts reached North America. Strabo in his Geographia, says:

"Among all the tribes there are three classes of men held in special regard: the Bards, the Ovates and the Druids. The Bards are singers and poets, the Ovates interpreters of sacrifice and natural philosophers, while the Druids, in addition to the science of nature, also study moral philosophy. They are the most just of men..."

Diodorus Siculus gives the same classification. The division of the intellectual classes of Ireland into Drui, File and Baird supports the existence of this structure universally within the Druid Order. In turn this leads to my own argument that the Druid Order was the instrument of intellectual leadership that held in peace the insular Celts of Ireland and Britain together with those of Gaul, acting as a Triple Order. The harassment by that great Irish High King, Niall of the Nine Hostages, of the Roman outposts of Britain and France in aid of the native British and Gaulish Celts is a late example of this Druidic triple alliance in action. At one time he reportedly sailed up the Seine and reached as far as Paris in pursuit of the fleeing Romans.

Reverence for Rome has ensured that this heroic Irish warlord, locked in combat with the decaying Roman Empire, never received the recognition he deserved as he is supposed to be responsible for the abduction of the young Patrick and has suffered much unfair historical vilification as a result.

We are more than we appear to be. The world is more than it appears to be. Mankind, generally speaking, is very limited in its awareness of what is really going on. Druidry is an attempt to work at the edges of it, to find out more about what we are. There is an overall meaning to everybody's existence, which is the constant cycle of living, dying, corning back. We are headed somewhere - back to where we came from initially, when we were perfect in a very real sense.

"There was in those days a great king and his seat was at Tara. He had around him his wise men the Druids, fortune tellers and sorcerers, and the inventors of the secret craft who were able to know everything before it happened. Two of them prophesied that a new way of life was about to arrive from overseas, with an unheard-of and burdensome teaching, which would overthrow kingdoms, kill kings who resisted it, banish all the works of their magic art and reign forever."

Druidry teaches the path of freedom and self-determination, as distinct from obedience to the written word and the priesthood, offering a radically different challenge to humanity.

THE MAGIC OF TREES AND GROVES.

After reading that classic by Watkins The Old Straight Track in 1949, Tony Wedd took a walk across Parliament Hill to Highgate Ponds:

"Turning there towards Ken Wood and climbing up the slope, I spotted a solitary Scots pine tree among the beeches: 'A mark!' I called ecstatically. It stood a clear ten feet above the other trees, like a flag on top of a fortress, its mushroom structure always pressing for the extra light due to its extra height.

"It often seems to me that the lay of the land itself reveals the angle from which a mark is meant to be approached. So, as I stood there on Hampstead Heath, I felt that it was just from that point of view that the single surviving Pinus Sylvestris was intended to be seen. With what delight, therefore, on scanning the surroundings on the Heath did I spot barely fifty yards to my left - the Tumulus! There is only the one, topped by Pinus Sylvestris, and encircled by a crown of thorns."

Upon plotting the line on the map he found that it passed straight through Westminster Abbey, standing on the site originally called Thorney Island because of an outstanding mark - a hallowed clump of hawthorn.

One of the most conspicuous marks Tony Wedd ever found to fall into alignment with others was Gill's Lap, high on Ashdown Forest. This was marvellously described by A.A. Milne in The House on Pooh Corner:

They walked on thinking of This and That, and by-the-by they came to an enchanted place on the very top of the forest called Galleon's Leap, which is sixty-something trees in a circle; and Christopher Robin knew that it was enchanted because nobody had ever been able to count whether it was sixty-three or sixty-four, not even after he had tied a piece of string around each tree after he had counted it. Being enchanted, its floor was not like the floor of the forest, gorse, bracken and heather, but close-set grass. It was the only place in the forest where you could sit down carelessly without getting up again almost at once and looking for somewhere else. Sitting there they could see the whole world spread out until it reached the sky, and whatever there was all the world over was with them there in Galleon's Leap.

Taken as a description of a Druidic grove, this has never been surpassed. Druidic groves in England are to be found in Somerset and Wiltshire to the present day, based on the presence of most of the trees described by Robert Graves in his The White Goddess as forming the Celtic tree alphabet and tree calendar, a real guide to the presence of a grove. The trees were recognised and known by local folk to be sacred, and these wise people tended them and ensured their survival.

This practice of tending to the grove was undertaken by certain traditional families and communities, right into our present time, using 'bygone' ritual to maintain the subtle energies of the grove as well as the physical features. But it is dying out and one of our particular roles in the Druid Order is to continue safeguarding and tending to the trees as occurs to us best. There was a continuous instinctive replanting of the right trees in the groves, and keeping others out. Some of the groves have survived better than others, like our own Marble City Grove, because the energies are right, thus enabling some groves such as our own of Kilkenny to survive from the more distant past.

Well we know what the sensitive Dorothy MacLean did above in Findhorn in Scotland, tuning into nature spirits and following the insights thus gained, the spirit-perfumed garden flourished - to the amazement of the unknowing, among the sand dunes.

The dowser Havelock Fiddler divined that the Scots pine acts as an interrupter of earth energy lines and it is in this way that trees can draw out and absorb disease from afflicted persons. Thus it was in ancient times that sick people went out to draw on the energies of the trees.

The Druidic groves acted, drawing up earth energies and releasing them into people and animals. Druids draw these energies in the groves into crystals and release them from the crystals into people and animals curing many maladies and diseases. AE the Druid was aware of the earth spirit and seemed consciously to tune into 'earth memories' and the 'memory of nature'.

John Mitchell clarified:

"The ways between these places ...are ways of the earth spirit, not merely secular routes but natural channels of energy, first traced out by the creative gods, followed by the primeval wandering tribes and still in settled times used by religious processions or pilgrims to a shrine. Traditionally they are also the paths of psychic apparitions, spirits of the dead or fairies, particularly on one day of the year. People of the Irish countryside recognise certain lines, unmarked on the ground, as fairy paths, lines of a seasonal flow of spirit which must on no account be obstructed or built upon."

Ian Taylor writes of the building of churches as simply a continuation of the Druidic groves:

"Christian churches were modelled upon them, the pillars and the arches representing the trunks and bows of the sacred forest. Pre-Reformation churches were painted in imitation of the colours of the woodland, from which gods and elementals looked out upon the worshippers."

The Chinese practice of Feng Shui can be complimented by the energy-control sciences of the Druids. John Mitchell pointed out:

"Not that the early wandering people needed any formal system of Feng Shui, because they lived and moved under the direct influence of the earth's subtle energies. Its principles were naturally integrated in their lives. Like all sciences Feng Shui is an expedient of civilisation, a technique for reconciling human nature to the limits imposed upon it by settlement."

Harmonisation of earth energies consists of a whole range of landscape modifications. Mounds might be raised. Trees might be planted on earthworks thrown up to the north of your home to dispel harmful energies emanating from that quarter. Ponds with gently flowing water and artificial waterfalls might be inlaid or existing streams banked up and diverted.

Then the ancient Druidic science of balancing your local earth energies into symmetrically flowing patterns of purity in which all life forms grow perfectly, could be employed. A rowan tree could be planted strategically, rock crystals placed to advantage too.

I have tended our local Druid Well of Kenny, still flowing today perhaps from the beginning of time. It belonged to the Druids on the mound a couple of hundred yards away. It feeds into the little meandering river Breagach, the False One, so named because in flood it can end up almost anywhere, usually through the nearby Black Abbey. A Norman bishop gave the old Druid well to the Dominicans there in the thirteenth century and it seems as if it is still intent on flooding them out.

Chapter Thirteen

Shaman, Druid and King

The Lord of the Rings breathes the very atmosphere of the Celtic Otherworld and even has Druids in the form of the magicians Gandulf and Saroman. The magic school of the Harry Potter stories has its basis in the ancient colleges of the Druids and much of the success of these stories and films of spellcraft and wizardry is due to their appeal to adults just as our Druidic mythology held everybody spellbound at the courts of the kings. Merlin is the inspiration for all.

According to Jean Markale the Druids chose yew and rowan for their wands. They also used hazel, which is the tree associated with wisdom in Celtic lore and with which the traditional diviner's rod was made. Druidry has a shamanic component. The shaman can be defined as one who acquired an extraordinary rapport with and mastery over the environment in its natural and more importantly its supernatural aspects. The shaman especially acquires the gift of inducing trances during which he leaves his mortal body. He also gains the powers of prophecy, clairvoyance and clairaudience. In trance he visits the spirit world to negotiate on behalf of his fellows. The induction of trance was often aided by the taking of hallucinatory drugs. After repeated visits to the Otherworld the shaman enters special relationship with one of those who dwells there and which becomes the guardian spirit of the tribe. In time the shaman enters that Otherworld at death and becomes the spirit of the new succeeding shaman, and so, on and on.

With the entrance of evil spirits, or even worse, witches, the shaman uses his influence in the Otherworld to banish them to the nether regions. Thus the Druidic world had its duality of good and evil. With his powers to banish the evil spirits of illness and disease the shaman becomes the healer. And with his unique knowledge of the Otherworld the Shaman is called upon to guide the spirits of the newly dead through the realms of the spirit world. It is the commencement of priesthood. All faith, all religion is based on finding ways around the finality of death. The antiquity of the shaman is shown to go back 20 to 30 thousand years in the cave drawings such as the famous Sorcerer of Les Trois Freres in Southern France. He is found all over the world.[1]

The ancient Irish at such sacred places as Newgrange, Knowth and Dowth preserved the bones of their departed gods in that great Necropolis of the Boyne. Michael Hamer devotes a chapter of his book The Way of the Shaman, in effect a do-it yourself manual on how to become a shaman, to 'power animals' said to inhabit the shaman and act as his guardian spirits. Rob Stewart claims such power animals for Merlin.

Although there is a shamanistic component to Druidry that is all it is. To attribute a coherent body of intellectual, moral and ethical wisdom to shamanism, as is attributed to Druidry, would be to totally misunderstand its nature. Yet there is so much in common. To become a shaman the novice trains almost all his life at the feet of an elder. All teaching is oral. The shaman's function as mediator with the spirit world gives him immense power and prestige, so much so that he may become chief. He is usually found out in the wilderness, close to nature, and his companions are the birds and the animals with whom he is able to communicate.

Here too he finds his Anam Cara, his soul friend, who is sprite or animal or both. Today that soul friend is usually a Druid, as John O'Donoghue hints from beginning to end of his best-selling books "Anam Cara" The shaman's soul journey involves crossing a turbulent river, the frontier between two worlds, usually by way of a dangerous narrow bridge:

We have thrown a bridge, of at first only a few worn strands, across a yawning dark and dangerous chasm, blasted to and fro in lashing wild gale winds, and somehow, some of us have hung on grimly for dear life as we crossed, painfully, excruciatingly slowly, slipping, sliding, inching, blown and tossed about pitifully like rag dolls in places, clambering across vast arches of time spanning fifteen hundred years, hitchhiking gladly for parts of the way from bronzed charioteers. But we have seen it, and all that is behind it, and we have brought it back across the centuries for man to know, and perhaps to die having known. What of it? For we have seen that we were giants in the Earth and that we will be again as we throw a few strands up into the golden sun-calmed clear blue heavens. For now we evolve into the future to create ourselves once more.

In Otherworld all things are the mirror image of our own. Right becomes left. It is day there when it is night here. For this reason most shamanic practices of the Druids take place in the hours of darkness. White Wicca comes from the black shamanism of Mother Earth. It is possible to trace the shaman behind many beliefs. Wandering spirits are capable of taking up residence in bodies and wombs. Thus is reincarnation traced. And the shamanism that gave rise to Druidry goes back six thousand years, probably further.

Since the otherworld lies so close to our own - there were gods rather than fairies at the bottom of the Celtic garden - it is only necessary to visit a charged place like Tara and sleep there to enter it. But, unlike the shaman's, the Druid's Otherworld is not the Underworld of the Dead.

The missionaries who arrived to convert us at the beginning of the fifth century tell us nothing of our Druids. There is at least a strong hint that the Church saw the Druids as an intellectual force to be reckoned with. Far from being renowned for learning it was the ignorance of the converting monks that was proverbial.

A few centuries later Ireland was known as the "Island of Saints and Scholars" whose missionaries had meanwhile gained an international reputation. They must have learned much, especially in training the memory, in oratory, in mathematics, astronomy and decorative art from the native intellectuals of Ireland, the Fili, Ovates and Druids.

In England the great Druidess Queen Boadicea -"Bua Dica" (Victory, I Say!) was probably the last of the great British Celtic monarchs. After she had wiped out a couple of Roman legions following upon the Roman sacking of the Druidic holy island of Anglesey, Britain more or less settled down to become in time the happiest of Christian Roman provinces.

From the year 410 onwards, as the Romans and Romano-British legions withdrew from the British Island to defend the centre of the Empire, the Scottish and Pictish raids grew more daring than ever. Soon these were added too by incursions across the North Sea until in 446 AD an impassioned plea was made for help to Rome. Unable to provide forces the emperor made provision for the organisation of local defence forces. This was done in different ways.

One way was that employed by the king of the Cantii whose name has come down to us as King Vortigem. In fact Vortigern - 'Mor Tighearna' in Irish - is not a name but a title meaning 'Great Lord'. He called the Saxons into his Kentish kingdom to aid him. The Saxons, led by Hengist and Horsa flooded into Kent and ousted Vortigern from his kingdom. It was the beginning of the successful Anglo-Saxon invasion of England and its resistance by the Celtic Christian King Arthur aided by Merlin and the forces of the Old religion. Incidentally the wise folk who acted as advisers to the Anglo-Saxon invaders were known as the Wiccans, who from that time on became the implacable foes of the Druids and the Celts. Indeed it can be considered that from this time onwards in England the Druid and the Christian began to share common ground.

At the start, however, Romano-British Christians disliked Vortigern because he was a pagan king who kept Druids and therefore they regarded him as a reactionary.

According to Geoffrey of Monmouth, Vortigem's Chief Druid or magician was Merlin, fatherless because his mother conceived him after being seduced from the Otherworld. However all Vortigern's attempts failed and the Saxon invasion continued. His son, also known by his title Vortemir or 'Great Commander', also resisted the Saxon invasion but was driven relentlessly back to the west.

This brings us to the consideration of the historical rather than the mythical king. One theory is that Arthur was a professional Roman commander named Artorius who, after the Roman withdrawal, hired out his services to British kings, probably as the leader of a mercenary cavalry unit. Highly mobile, this unit was able to meet the Saxon threat wherever it appeared.

The two earliest references to Arthur, in the Annales Cambriae and Nennius. which mention the Battle of Mount Badon do not describe him as a king. In the first report he is not even mentioned, but Nennius revealingly describes him as Dux Bellorum, which to those few of us still with Latin means "the leader of war" or War Leader. This is in keeping with Celtic custom and tradition. Where a war is being fought that requires all of the Celtic tribes to fight it, a battle for survival against invasion, they elected an overall leader of the combined tribes who would have such a title as War Leader, and this is what Dux Bellorum was. In more ancient times, to avoid jealousy, and to bring great power upon their arms, one of the gods would have been named as king while a conclave of tribal leaders would have chosen the earthly general needed as the divine chief-of-staff. In these mixed religious times, as between the Christians and the followers of the Old Religion no god would have been chosen. So, in reality Arthur would have been king in all but coronation - and that probably followed in celebration of his first early victories, carried out by Christian priest and the Druid, Merlin. The site of the Battle of Mount Badon, mentioned in the Annales and Nennius remains uncertain, although Bath is the likely site. The outcome of that battle temporarily halted the Saxon invasion. The British Celts, although confined to the west behind a fortified line, enjoyed twenty years of peace.

If the historical Arthur ever held power, the Round Table held sway in the west of Britain during these years.

This was the nearest the Celts of Britain ever came to united nationhood during their entire history. The climax of his dynastic quarrel with Mordred, in which both of them were killed, came at Camlann, and the way was open for the Saxons to complete their conquest.

Geoffrey Ashe provides one of the latest and most plausible identifications of Arthur in his The Discovery of King Arthur. Ashe identifies him with 'Riothamus', obviously derived from the Celtic word 'Rigotamus' meaning 'The Great King' - a British ruler who led an army into Gaul in the fifth century and who may have died at Avallon in Burgundy.
Arthur had a royal court at Kelliwic in Cornwall, while the Battle of Camlann also took place there. His Christian credentials could be examined. Annales Cambriae states that during the battle the leader carried the cross of 'Our Lord Jesus Christ' for three days and three nights, and Nennius says that he carried the image of the Virgin Mary on his shoulder, but this may be the wishful thinking of monkish scribes. He is supposed to be a devout Christian king but when we look beneath all the superficial pious declarations we get a whiff of the powerful druidic prince. He is intimately associated with Merlin, as much entitled to be called a Druid as anybody at Vortigem's court. It was Merlin's magic that enabled Arthur's father, Uther Pendragon, to seduce Igema (Ighema or Ieme -Ireland!) . At Merlin's insistence the son of that union established his right to the throne, by the test of the sword in the stone. There is his queen Guinevere. She has an Irish counterpart in 'Finnabair', daughter of Meabh of Connaught, certainly a goddess, while, according to Mallory, Guinevere was the daughter of Sir Leodegrance, generally taken to be a corruption of Ogyr Vran, another form for the name of the Celtic god Bran.

She begins to look less like a mortal wife than one of those divine beings to whom, in druidic times, the king was ritually married.

This goes some way in explaining why the Glastonbury epitaph refers to her as 'second wife' because druidic kings did indeed have two wives - one mortal, one immortal. There is considerable support for the Queen of Camelot's Otherworld nature. In Chrétien de Troyes Perceval, Arthur's mother asks Gawain about Guinevere at the Castle of the Miracle. He replies that the Queen of Camelot teaches every living being and that she is the origin and font of all that is good in the world. Another aspect typical of Celtic goddesses, that of La Belle Dame Sans Merci, is mentioned by Jean Frappier in his essay on Chretien deTroyes Lancelot or the Knight of the Cart. She treats her rescuer with icy scorn, refusing to show gratitude and even turning her back on him. Keats's poem La Belle Dame Sans Merci is based on the legend of the Irish Banshee, the beautiful Sidhe Women who, at Samhain, went in search of mortal lovers. Do they mean that Guinevere was a Woman of the Shee? Do we infer from this that Arthur fulfilled the Druidic royal rite of symbolically marrying the territorial goddess? Can this be reconciled with his reputation as a Christian prince? As a matter of tradition it can - Irish Christian kings carried out such symbolism, and a lot worse of a bestial nature, right into the middle ages. The stories of the Holy Grail went on to become a reflection of Druidry. Yet, today there are so many grails. The Holy Grail is even said to be the living body of the Magdalene, newly arrived in the Herodian estates in Southern France bearing Jesus Justus, the son of Jesus, in her womb.

There are several Merlins as well, two who can be readily identified. The patron saint of Glasgow is Kentigern, which, again, is not a name but the title 'Ceann Tighearna' meaning 'Head Lord', and a twelfth century life of this Kentigern mentions a madman called Laloecen.

A fifteenth century manuscript in the British Library (MS Cotton Titus, A xix) gives details: during a battle, warrior hosts began appearing in the sky. A man named 'Lailoken' was accused of being responsible for the slaughter of the battle (by the warrior hosts in the sky) and, as a result, went mad, deserted the habitations of men, and lived the life of a forest animal. St. Kentigern (St. Head Lord) learns the story when he meets him by chance just before the death he has prophesied for himself. This takes place when he is stoned and beaten by shepherds, impaled on a spike and thrown into the river Tweed, thus fulfilling his prophecy that he would die in three ways. 'Laloecen' and 'Lailoken' are misspellings of the Welsh word Llallogen which means "dear friend" and has been converted from a salutation into a name. In Geoffrey of Monmouth, Merlin is not mentioned after Arthur's conception, and it is not until the time of Robert de Boron at the turn of the twelfth century, that he becomes a permanent royal counsellor.

Nikolai Tolstoy sees Merlin, the Caledonian Forest madman, as a surviving relic of the past, associating him with the cults of gods like Kerne and Lugh and suggesting that he may have been a royal bard.

T.W. Rolleston, in Myths and Legends of the Celtic Race also associates Merlin with the god Nuada/Llud. This is further evidence, not only of the survival of the Druidic gods through the Roman era in Britain, but of a revival after the departure of the Romans.

Merlin's death in three ways recalls the Druidic triple death. The fact that Merlin's killers were shepherds is also significant in view of the fact that the old ways survived most tenaciously among country people.
His death appears to be a ritual sacrifice in which he is the willing victim. This would explain how he was able to predict his own triple death so accurately.

Merlin leaves us with huge unanswered questions: the manner of his birth, life and death can be equated with that of Jesus - his birth by a virgin mother impregnated from the spirit world, his life spent in magic, his death a ritual sacrifice.

As a Druid he finally offered his life in the sacrifice of the triple death for the triumph of the Kingdom of Arthur. Today it looks like he succeeded, how well you may say.

Divination

Chapter Fourteen

Druid Divination

The desire to learn about, foretell and receive assurance from the future has been with us since the beginning of time. Among the very original practitioners were the Druids. Today we have many more tellers of the future: weather forecasters, economists, insurance actuaries, sports commentators, bookies, horoscope and tarot lines and so on. Many of us have a go ourselves. This seems a fair bet as psychologists say that we use only ten percent of our brain and that we have abilities and areas of the brain that lie dormant and untapped for most of our lives. Divination is as old as man. Diviners have appeared in every culture, from the oracles of classical Greek civilization and Tibet to today's online computer-based tarot forecasts with names based on the word "Celtic" in particular, as if such activities have anything to do with the Druids. Our Druids used dowsing, astrology, geomancy, clairvoyance, water and sky scrying and ogham sticks. Druidry today combines modern methods with ancient wisdom, and this section has fascinating insights from our tradition not to be found anywhere else.

The Druids divined from lying on their backs and gazing intently into the clouds above, just as they could tell the future from gazing intently into the flames of festival fire on a sacred site.

Above all they divined from the spirits of the dead.

Persons wishing to train as Druid astrologers today should first undergo the usual four years of astrological studies and become adept as astrologers before they undertake Druidic astrological studies. It is self-evident that a Druid astrologer should first be a Druid. This is usually achieved today by associating with a reputable Druid Order in the world. The Order of Druids in Ireland has a great reputation indeed for the quality of its starlore.

Needless to say, out of respect for themselves and their future clients, all wishing to become adept astrologers of any kind should first undertake basic astronomy and the required mathematics, to be followed up at a later stage with cosmology if they are truly dedicated. The Irish Astrological Association publishes the very best journal I have come across called Realta - Stars.

In all, if it is of any consolation to the reader who wishes to become a Druid astrologer, I would reckon upon a timescale from scratch of about seven years to get there. In academic terms the grade Druid astrologer is equivalent to a Ph.D in a tough science subject such as relativistic cosmology.

In ancient Ireland the Archdruids and Chief Druids were chosen mostly from the ranks of the Druid astronomer/astrologers.

If you don't fancy such hard gruelling years of study you may alternatively take up some of the easier options in the other divinations, in treelore or in certain healing arts if you feel so gifted. Or you could qualify as a Druid in charge of ritual and ceremonial. You may have a gift for pendulum dowsing, geomancy, hypnotherapy or even tarot, which is today practised by most Druids although there is no evidence that the ancient Druids ever used the cards. Painstaking work is being done in trying to rediscover the true Druidic astrology. usually referred to as Starlore. So rapid is our progress in this determination that I have had to strike out some paragraphs that I had written here with great confidence and assurance only last year, because they are already out of date!. We may not have the exact Druid science yet but we are getting there,, "

Robert Graves later admitted that in his extraordinary book The White Goddess he made some mistakes and educated guesses and indeed he did. The thirteen- month year of twenty-eight days that he postulated for the ancient Druids, exciting as it was, now looks to be wide of the mark.
The Coligny Calendar looks more than ever to be the true calendar of the Celts, and by extension of our ancient Druids.
Samhain as the end of the Celtic Year is now just a fanciful wiccanry. Was it ever else?

Graves based his researches on Ogygia by Roderick O'Flaherty, on the Celtic tree alphabet, which Graves and others considered to be a genuine relic of Druidry orally transmitted down through the ages. And in treelore Graves does have a level of credibility not achieved by any others. The Midwinter Solstice is the death and rebirth of the Druidic Year when the sacred rays of the reborn sun stream through the window box at Newgrange for seventeen minutes, lighting up the sacred chamber of Ireland with the new light of the pyramids a couple of thousand miles away to the south, symbolising a reunion of the one ancient knowledge and wisdom.

Classical scholar and poet Robert Graves in his foreword to The White

Goddess affirms his own Celtic bloodline when he writes:
"English poetic education should begin not with the Canterbury Tales, not with the Odyssey, and not even with Genesis, but with the Song of Amergin (pronounced Aweverrgeen), an ancient Celtic calendar alphabet and Druidic incantation which summarises a prime poetic myth relating not only to their ancestral origins, but to our own."

There are references to actual astrological divination in the ancient Irish manuscripts, such as that performed by the Druid Cathbad at the birth of Deirdre. Mog Ruith operated his magic with the aid of a great wheel. Outside of the Druids, we read astrology in the Dead Sea Scrolls of the Essenes at Qum'ran.

BEYOND THE TRIPLE SPIRAL

That marvellous conjunction with the sun aligned to the galactic centre at the winter solstice, enshrined for over five thousand years at Newgrange in Ireland is a fabulous piece of guesswork if we are to believe those who still fanatically maintain that our ancestors were mere pagan shamen!
For this astronomical alignment has only in recent years been confirmed by modern science in the persons of the noted astronomers Stromberg, Wilson and More. The triple spiral etched onto the stones of Newgrange represents nothing less than drawings of far-off galaxies invisible to the naked human eye.
Now you know what Blake meant when he wrote: " The ancients saw it in the heavens and wrote it upon the Earth." They say the Druids left no books. Others say that Patrick and his missionaries burned hundreds of them. There are many books of the Druids left upon the Earth in the form of thousands of standing stones, circles, dolmens and cairns left across the face of Ireland, Britain and northwest Europe. All you have to do is learn to read them, the stones below and the stars above, and they will speak volumes to you.

UNDER THE STARRY SKY

The Druid watched under the starry sky. He observed certain stars. The blue star Vega is aligned to several stone circles. He watched the Pleiades whose rising is aligned to the Heol Stone at Stonehenge. He gazed at Altair at the cusp of Aquarius, the major star of the constellation Aquila the Eagle which forms part of the Milky Way. The Druids looked upon the Milky Way as the great star-serpent Sarph representing the Primum Mobile, the origin of all things. Altair, Capella, Cygnus are important.

In Druidic astrology Altair is courageous and liberal, associated in the birth chart with sudden but fleeting wealth. The Druid sees his familiar star Deneb in the last decan of Aquarius in the constellation of Cygnus the Swan where God alone exists and cosmologists posit a black hole in space. From this primeval darkness the Druid is again emerging as the cosmologist par excellence.

It may be of significance too that Cygnus is in the shape of a cross in the heavens, known through the centuries as the Northern Cross, a guide to the ancient mariner and to worlds beyond too. In the centre of Gemini is the brilliant Druidic star Rigel in the constellation of Orion the Hunter, which can confer great military honours. Gemini, one of the brightest constellations, is aligned to several ancient Druidic observatories.

The Druid sees the star Castor lose his power at the Midsummer Solstice. Nearby is Bellatrix, named after a Gaulish God, known to confer the greatest military honours, but ending in gotterdammerung! The stars Pollux and Procyon represent another twin star element in Druidic cosmology. Pollux, the immortal twin of Castor, represents the evergreen spirit. In Druidic starlore Pollux symbolises the Celtic martial arts as well. The Druid sees Procyon in Canis Minor of Carris Major as representative of the Egyptian occult star Sirius.

The Druid watches Sirius, the dog star, brightest in the sky, on the sacred south horizon of white fire at the Midwinter Solstice. The Druid gathers his powerful plants at the rising of Sirius, which is the Druidic star of healing, so vital and sacred to the ancient Egyptians too. If there is a conjunction of sun or moon with Procyon in the birth chart then the native is a natural healer. In ancient starlore Spica is regarded as one of the most fortunate of stars when rising in the midheaven, offering riches and renown.

Arcturus is one of the brightest stars in the northern sky, prominent there from spring to autumn when it finally falls below the horizon. Druids identify it with the legendary King Arthur, and its annual rise and fall symbolise his.

The west coast of Munster in Ireland was regarded by the ancient Druids to be the primeval place of creation from whence all earth life evolved. This primeval origin was referred to by all Celts as the Great Deep, and their ancient title of "People of the Sea", conferred upon them by the ancient Egyptians, is regarded by some as claiming Atlantean origin. Visions of

Mog Ruith descending from Atlantis upon his most westerly island of Valentia off the coast of Kerry spring up.

I position the northernmost island of Atlantis as ninety miles distant from Valentia out into the Atlantic along the major east-west ley line across Ireland at latitude 51.42 degrees, the circle divided by seven, the magical angle of the Pyramids! The Atlantis Line is the culmination of all the Druidic sciences and practices I describe.

Importantly you are now equipped to explore the secrets independently, on your own, so as to eventually find the wisdom of the Druids. Pluto in modem Druidic cosmology represents the penultimate darkness. The solar deity Arthur, the Irish King Airim, yearly descended into the abyss off the Munster coast to rescue souls trapped and unable to reincarnate.
In esoteric astrology Pluto represents the void, the Sea of Daath of the Qabalah.The descent into the abyss represents "the dark night of the soul", a crossing of the astral sea, a shattering cataclysmic experience which finally liberates the spiritual kingdom within. The Druids clearly understood this liberating spiritual process of individual evolution, this 'rising upon the plains' until one is a Druid-Magus and finally an Ipsissimus, On the Tree of Life the demon Choronzon guards passage across the Sea of Daath. To cross over to the elect of the Supernal Triad you must elude or defeat him. In the heavens he is Antares, the bright red star of the Sagittarian degrees, but belonging to the constellation of Scorpio.
To the ancient Druids he is the 'Watcher of the West', the deputy of Mars with a malevolent side.
To defeat him you must defeat the malevolent side within yourself every day, every night, for six moons from the Vernal Equinox to the Autumnal Equinox , commencing in purity under the guidance of a Master and the protection of the Guardian. For this is the path of High Druidry.

THE FESTIVALS AND THE STARS

Wiccans and other pagans generally assign to the four Druidic festivals the following dates: Imbolg, 1st February; Bealtaine, 1st May; Lughnasadh, 1st August; Samhain, 1st November. This is basic, far too simplified, displaying a lack of knowledge of how the times and dates of the Druidic festivals were and are computed. Indeed the sixth days of February, May, August and November would be a little more accurate as these dates fall roughly halfway between the equinoxes and the solstices.

Midwinter, or the winter solstice, marks the beginning of the Druidic Year. The precise date was, and is, easily calculated. If in doubt the "window box" is there at Newgrange in Ireland to check. Your local observatory will give you the exact second of the birth of the new year at the winter solstice, also the exact point of the midsummer solstice, and the equinoxes.

In the death of the year there is the rebirth and throughout the darkness of the longest night we await the dawn of the birth of the new year. At the celebration of the midwinter solstice we extinguish our lights, face the southeast, and await the first faint glow, the first glimmer, of the rays of the newborn sun on the horizon as we prepare ourselves for the dawning of the day.

Imbolg, or La le Feile Brighde, the day of the Festival of Brigid, Triple Goddess: Earth Mother, Lady of Alchemy, and Goddess of Bardic Art. I disagree with those who surmise that the winter festivals were held indoors. There had to be an outdoor celebration after sunset on the eve of the festivals. We hardier types of Irish Druids prefer to celebrate all the festivals outdoors throughout the year, hail, rain or snow. A shaman would never mark any festival indoors! But you may of course hold the winter festivals indoors as it's better than not holding them at all. Imbolg was of little interest to the Druids, being a festival of the Daor, the slaves and common folk.

I would naturally love to complicate matters even further by introducing all phases of the moon and planetary positions into the 'equations' of fixing the festival dates. But the journalist in me gets the upper hand in simplifying matters. Bealtaine was held in "the horns of the moon" under a waxing crescent, Lughnasadh under the full moon and Samhain at the waning last quarter as the veil between this and the underworld was lifted. The gravitational pull on the earth is strongest during a full moon, with the sun and moon pulling on the earth from opposite directions, giving rise to an energetic phase of the telluric force. Gravitational pull on the Earth would be as powerful at the time of the new moon, but it is unidirectional and I refuse to believe that the Celts, or any other ancient people, would have celebrated their festivals at the terrible time of 'No Moon in the Sky'. Many occultists need to commence certain magical operations at the new moon, highly dangerous for those not of the grade. But the festivals were big public ceremonies for the entire population, and I think people would have been a bit browned off celebrating under dark moonless skies.

The Vernal Equinox, or Spring Equinox, is within a few days of Patrick's Day.

The earth opens with delight. With Colmcille the Half Druid and Brighid the Goddess, Druidry can claim much of the Irish saintly pantheon.

Bealtaine in Taurus the Bull, naturally, under the constellation of Perseus, is everybody's festival the world over, the start of summer when we happily trudge off into the hills and light the Bealtaine May fires.

The Midsummer Solstice. The Archdruid, the Provincial Archdruids, the Druids and Druidesses celebrate the midsummer solstice at noon on June 21st upon the royal and ancient hill of Tara. Dedicated types are up all night on the hill to welcome and cheer in the dawn of the solstice. Religious denominations simply fade away for all that they matter into the Tara air. Participants and spectators alike get up onto the central mound to say what they like.

No person can be interrupted as he or she speaks to the assembly. For it is the Druid way to stand or sit silently and listen to perhaps an unexpected word of wisdom from a stranger. And we have been delighted to hear several such nuggets. Then, the Noon Ceremonial is over, but, no, not the day! After visits to Dowth, Knowth and Newgrange across the nearby Boyne Valley, it's in through Drogheda for the evening and back to Dublin by nightfall for more music, poetry, song, dance into the small hours.

Lughnasadh in Leo under the constellation of Ursa Major when the Order celebrates within its own groves.
My Marble City Grove holds the ceremonial within our own grove and stone circle along the banks of the river Nore. There are visits to the nearby Mound of the Guardian and our still flowing Druidic Well.

Autumn Equinox is a time of the last rose of summer, time for order, for taking stock as we see many of our companions and friends for the last time in the year.

Samhain under Draco the dragon, is not the end of the year and the beginning of another, as the Wiccans hold - that's the Midwinter solstice as evidenced at Newgrange.
"Many things about the nature of things, the stars and the immortal Gods", declares Julius Caesar about the Druidic wisdom. The ancient books of Wales describe these, and one dominant plan of the heavens based upon the work of the Irish philosopher John Scotus Eriugena (810 - 877 AD), who was a major chronicler of Irish Druidic wisdom. The Book of Taliesin

implies that each grade of Druid had its proper astronomical study: the Druids themselves the fixed stars, the Bards the planets and the Ovates the spiritual intelligence of the night.

Chapter Fifteen

Revelation. A Druid reects on Tarot

"What thou seest write in a book and send it unto the seven abodes that are in Assiah."
"And I saw in the right hand of Him that sat upon the throne a book sealed with seven seals. And I saw a strong angel proclaiming with a loud voice, 'Who is worthy to open the Book and loose the seals thereof '"

Tarot, the Book of Thoth, did it come out of ancient Egypt? If it did then the Druids knew of it and some of them might have used it. I like to think so because I like tarot. I like to use it, to play with a deck, to concentrate on the cards, to contemplate, to speculate, to visualise. They are indeed High Magic's Aid. I usually have them by me.

Yes, I would like to think the ancient Druids used tarot too. The cards have told me so much about myself, about my friends, about almost everything, and give me, as well as countless millions of people today so much joy and pleasure. Tarot has happily passed away quiet hours for me. I am never bored as long as I have a deck. I quickly become immersed. The tarot is such an ideal partner, in a bus, on a train, in a hotel room, or just passing the time away at home on a wintry wet Irish Sunday afternoon.

Sadly, I don't think that the ancient Druids had the tarot. I am open to correction. But don't let that put you off.

Some Druids of the middle ages did. Many of the later Fili did. And the Druids who led the 18 th century revival definitely used tarot. Most Druids I know use the tarot. Millions of wiccans, new agers and pagans do as well. So do millions of Christians! I know that when I read most modem Druid books I am disappointed, as you are, because there is nothing about tarot. This is strange as nine out of ten Druids use tarot, many of them veritable masters of the cards.

As a Druid you should hit a question with everything you've got - Astrology, Tarot, Dowsing, Scrying etc. Use science and logic, meditation and visualisation too. Be a real general practitioner. The more psychic and occult aids you can bring to bear the better. Use your mind for a change, hypnotherapy and Neuro linguistic Programming, versions of which were used by the Druids, techniques being introduced, or re-introduced into Druidry today. Lie on your back and divine by the sky and the clouds, as the Nealadoir (pronounced 'nail-a-door'), the Druid astrologer did. Stare into the flames of the fire and see the patterns of the flames and what they are telling you.

Comfortably resting your arm on the bridge, gaze down into the river and see what it tells you. Try Yoga. , relaxation, mantras, and only when you are ready, magical ritual too. Cosmology is a powerful tool of the mind - it kept Stephen Hawking alive for forty years more than the doctors said. Keep your mind as well as your body active. Have a lifelong interest and your life will be longer and more enjoyable too.

Give up tap water with its fluorine (poisoning the brain) and chlorine (poisoning the body). Walk to the well for spring water no matter how far away it is. day or night.

Take out the tarot and look at a card under the moon. In his Thoth deck Crowley names the Eight of Discs, as Prudence. This indicates that he firmly places the virtue Prudence in the minor Arcanum, and not being a prudent man he wants it to stay there.

The Seven of Discs is not the missing Tarot trump. It is a pointer of significance. It points to the missing trump. I therefore postulate that the Seven Seals of St. John represents the missing Tarot trump, which is the Apocalyptic Key or Revelation.

I do not , however, place the Apocalyptic Key physically in the Tarot trumps, although some may prefer to do so. It remains in the minor Arcanum represented by the Seven of Discs. We cannot, however, ignore it altogether in the major Arcanum. It is there. We allow for its influence. One satisfactory way to deal with the matter would be to set the Seven of Discs aside when it turns up in a reading, shuffle the deck, and replace the Discs Seven with the very first Tarot trump to turn up.

I have found that this makes for more accurate readings and more complete stories than the ordinary way. Another method is to rename the Seven of Discs as Revelation. Its name is not that of Wealth as ascribed to it by most commentators reading off other decks, but may be modified to Wealth Revealed - now you only have to go and find it! Reversed it may signify Festina Lente - hasten slowly along the path to Aladdin's Cave.

Some other cards of Druidic significances are as follows:

The Ace of Cups which is the Holy Grail. Or you may look upon it as the Druidic cauldron. This signifies victory for a leader in religion. For a religious leader or member of a mystical order, the Ace of Cups signifies a powerful new initiation.

The Ace of Swords: You are staring Excalibur straight in the face. The magical sword is yours for the time being. You now have the power to create a new order in your environment. Yours is the crown of Arthur.
His kingdom is yours and you cannot go wrong in it. For yours is the triumph of the will. For a political leader, politician or political aspirant the Ace of Swords signifies victory.

These two aces found together in a reading portend victory against all odds. They represent total mindpower. The mind is filled with the brilliance of a flash of lightning, replete with new insights, concepts and ideas. Should The Ace of Wands turn up in the same reading darkness is shattered. You know your mind. It knows itself. Your message will have a hypnotic effect on others. You gain a new mastery and enlightened understanding of the philosophies, religions and beliefs, and you know the strategies and tactics too. Ignorance is a thing of the past. Use your powers of knowledge and your insights of wisdom to the full.

The Ace of Swords is symbolic of the Great Rite. It is, as the sword enters the crown, the most powerful sexual symbol of the tarot. The Ace of Wands is the most phallic, and is also the highest energy card in the entire tarot after the Sun tarot, but it also signifies great spiritual and magical power -.the staff of the Druid.

Wield the Ace of Swords wisely or it shall be taken from you by the Lady of the Lake, in the form of the Queen of Cups. Guard yourself with the Ace of Discs for with this card you are given a magic shield, a shield for your journey through life at this time. In its general divinatory meaning the Ace of Discs indicates 'the good things in life', prosperity, benefits, winnings. It also represents the planet and the environment and points to success or failure in this field.

A few final points about the tarot for now. My own favourite pack, as you will have guessed by now, is the Crowley Thoth Tarot, and for a few compelling reasons. Crowley spent several years working on it together with his painter friend, Lady Frida Harris, not for any reasons of commercialism but as a labour of love based on expert knowledge.

The pack is also 'backed up' by the best tarot book in existence, The Book of Thoth by Crowley himself, and also by the very best guidebook to tarot readings, Mirror of the Soul, "Handbook for the Aleister Crowley Tarot" by Gerd Giegler, another labour of love that waxes lyrical, poetical and philosophical.

I use the Rider-Waite pack, the Marseille Deck and the Tarot of the Ages too. I will even use R.J. Stewart's Merlin Tarot if he wings it along to me, although I doubt if Merlin ever needed tarot, except possibly for amusement.

It is such a pity that the tarot is generally looked upon as a means of fortune telling. Tarot can bring you into realms way beyond mere divinatory use. As Eliphas Levi wrote:

"The tarot is a veritable oracle and replies to all possible questions with more precision and more infallibility than the android of Albertus Magnus. An imprisoned person with no other book than the tarot, if he knew how to use it, could in a few years acquire universal knowledge ..."

There are now hundreds of different packs, and hundreds of commentators coming up all the time with 'new ways' of spreading the cards. The writer has tried most of them - especially the Celtic cross spread - with interesting results.

It is best to learn how to place the cards on the Tree of Life, and, perhaps, even go on to learn a little tarot magic.

Tarot was never Druidic. But this is no reason why Druids today should miss out on the delightful worlds the cards open up. Tarot belongs to all.

Chapter Sixteen

Druidic Crystal Scrying

The Druids were masters of 'overseeing' by scrying. This is the occult art of seeing what another person is doing, where he or she is, whether as near as the next room, the house across the way, the shop down in the High Street, the hotel half a mile away, the castle a hundred miles away or a city on the other side of the country. Scrying is the art of divination by gazing into a reflective surface. To scry, you can use a clear stream or well, a vessel full of clear water, or best of all a natural rock crystal.

Druids prefer the rock crystal because of its intrinsic natural energy. Perfect specimens of rock crystal were difficult to obtain in the big cities such as Dublin, London, Paris and New York. So they made the crystal ball by the thousand and in time it became the most familiar symbol of the world of fortune telling and divination.

When you get your round of natural rock crystal, or your expensive new crystal ball, you will probably not see anything at first when you look into it. Only your own hands should ever touch your crystal. If anybody else touches it you will have to repeat your initial preparations and cleansing before you start the operation. The scrying ability is deep inside us so we must go deep inside ourselves to activate, bring forth and tap its latent ability. And as the images start to emerge you transform them into meaningful stories and predictions. You must get the crystal that suits you, the perfect one for you, that relates to your inner self, the perfect match. Such ideal matching is at the root of successful scrying.

You should make an appointment to spend some time in the shop, even bringing the crystal home on approbation if possible, to find your own matching 'inner crystal' through meditation and visualisation. The crystal that eventually relates to you will probably be a beryl or quartz sphere about four inches in diameter. If You choose to use a glass ball instead you should examine it to ensure that it is free from scratches and blemishes that would distract. To prepare the crystal, wash it in a solution of vinegar and water and polish it with a spotless white cloth devoted to this purpose only. Keep it wrapped in black velvet and stored in darkness well away from televisions, microwaves, mobile phones and the like when not in use. Direct sunlight is supposed to harm the sensitivity of the crystal but moonlight is supposed to be extremely beneficial so some scryers take their crystals out for a moon bath under the full moon.

Although the Druids preferred rock crystal for scrying, they probably used crystal balls too, as these were popularly used in Europe since the 5th century, and were probably employed earlier than this.

Before you start, bear in mind that most people see nothing in the crystal for their first fortnight of scrying. So don't worry if you don't see anything for a while. The path to crystal vision is bordered by patience and persistence. The room must be quiet. There must be no disturbance whatsoever. The light in the room should be like the light on a dull wet grey day. The crystal should be on its stand, or on a black velvet cushion. It must be surrounded by black velvet. At first it is best to be on your own to give your concentration a chance. After you have developed your powers then people may be allowed in to ask you questions in low voices. Sit comfortably in good heat and fix your eyes on the crystal in a steady calm gaze, but allow yourself to blink as normal, to be comfortable all round.

Keep the sessions to ten minutes at first, then a quarter of an hour, half an hour, but don't go over an hour.

CRYSTAL VISION

As the crystal begins to go dull and cloudy and as small points of light begin to appear as specks and then as tiny stars you are beginning to find your crystal vision. Then, in time, as you relax and breathe easily this cloudiness will begin to change into a blue ocean of space, something like the earth in space. After some more sessions and more time the vision will at last come clear as you see a tree, a bird, even people and you may see symbols like crosses for instance too.

Visions that appear in the background are from the distant past or the distant future while those nearer at hand in the foreground come from the present and the immediate future. Allow these images to come and go as they will so that more and more flow into you, past and around you as you relax and breathe easily.

I attach here a version of Francis Barrett's Scrying Manuscript that I adapted successfully for my own use. He it was the one who compiled and wrote "The Magus" in 1801. His scrying manuscript is the best available. I update it here for the modem scryer.

Francis Barrett was the author of The Magus (not to be confused with the modern novel by John Fowles). He is the enigmatic eighteenth century sorcerer whose work still influences occultists. Barrett was the first magician since the middle ages to compile a manual or a 'grimoire' of magic. His Magus or Celestial Intelligencer is probably only surpassed by Aleister Crowley's book, Magick in Theory and Practice.

You are probably searching for a copy of The Magus. Don't bother, it has been out of print for years, and whoever has it does not seem to be very excited about being in possession of a potential million-seller that everybody I know wants to buy regardless of the price! Barrett's parents came from Wales, probably Swansea, to London and he was born in Covent Garden -the magic garden again! The Garden has so much to do with the revival of Druidry over the past three hundred years.

Francis Barrett Senior was illiterate, a good Christian workman, but his wife Ann Jones, mother of 'the Magus', came from a long line of hereditary Welsh bards.

So Francis Barrett was of Welsh Druidic stock. To compile the Magus he borrowed the necessary occult books from John Denley, bookseller, who ran an occult shop at 10 Gate Street, Lincoln's Inn Fields, alongside Covent Garden. Bulwer-Lytton, who was a revivalist Druid, made Denley famous in his occult novel Zanoni. It is thought that Barrett, who was in his early thirties, was married with a child and after the Magus was published he disappeared from England. It is generally thought that he emigrated with his family to the United States.

THE SCRYING MANUSCRIPT

"Whoever attempts the invocation of spirits by a Crystal, let him pay due

Seamus Heaney speaks to save Tara Valley from the bulldozers. Photo by Anthony Murphy

Druids on Tara for the Midsummer Solstice

The Triple Spiral = An Biseach Triarach in the Irish language.

His father Mark was my friend and fellow photographer back in the 1970s in Kilkenny , where Ralph Fiennes lived as a teenager, we used to discuss history a lot back then.

SLEADY CASTLE, WEST WATERFORD, HOME OF THE CLANNA BUI McGRATH CLAN

Crest of the ancient city of Kilkenny where the author lives high up on the city hall - photographed by him.

Joyce was expert on the druids since he had lived near the sacred Hill of Uisneach as a boy, as Yeats expert, my former boss the late John Garvin explains in his book that I have, pictured here. I got to Know John Garvin when I was an Executive Officer in the Custom House, Dublin in 1965 when he was Secretary General of the Department of Local Government there.

attention to what is written here, which was written at the special desire of a friend whom I believe to be a sincere and true searcher into the mysterious operations of natural and spiritual magic.

The Crystal that is sent with this few pages of manuscript was consecrate by me, and made for my own particular use, and was shortly after lent by a lady aunt to a disciple of mine, who had conceived a particular desire to have the use of it for a few weeks, in the space of which time she had two particular visions, which satisfied her of the efficacy of magic, or the possibility of spirits appearing by this mode of invocation - having been favoured with the sight of spiritual agents she returned it to me again.
NB - Here follows the rights of ceremonies magical to be observed in all operations by Crystal and circle ...

Rules:

Before any man begins to use the agency of spirits he should first examine himself to be assured whether he is qualified for so sublime and heavenly a gift.

He must ask himself the following questions, viz. To what purpose do I determine to consult and draw spirits (whose nature I know nothing at all about) to myself?

Is it for the glory of God and the good of my neighbour? Or is it to enrich myself with monies and worldly treasures, with vainglory and fame, to get a name amongst men?
- Or is it to know seeing there are in this (Enlightened) Age so many who are ignobly ignorant, and who neither know/nor wish to know anything besides Eating and Drinking?

If, my friend your aim is knowledge, God give thee increase of wisdom for if a man was born on a dunghill if he desires to know, that man is worth a million of men who carry fine cloaks on their back and their heads in their pockets. There is nothing better for a man in a humble or high sphere than wisdom - how is it to be obtained; by seeking -by loving God - by fearing him - by endeavouring to mend our heart - by loving the outcast of mankind, the poor, the humble, the needy, the afflicted, the unfortunate!

What is Christianity? Where is its Glory? Is it in the practice do we love one another? We do that desire wisdom, we love one another. Therefore mere

Christianity is deficient as it is practiced - but philosophy enforces us to follow the precepts, which is to seek the Kingdom of God and all the rest you shall have When a man thoroughly enters into himself he shall find first that he is entirely deficient without the aid of God and without a soul, (without) a firm dependence on Him he can never bring any wonderful thing to pass - although Necromancers affirm they can do miracles (so they think).

The Devil, having a certain limited power, can infuse himself into the souls of men and being joined thereto can work many (seeming) wonderful effects - but they are mere illusions, nor can truth belong to them -therefore it is better that a man had never been born than that he should be inveigled by an evil spirit.

Therefore desire not to see any evil spirit whatever but desire to see and converse with a good spirit, either by Crystal or dream, or by inspiration and desire that you may be informed by the spirit what is best for thee to pursue whether Physic (or healing) or teaching others or alchemy or herbs or prophecy (which is the greatest) or anything else that might please God to call thee to, for every man hath his appointed end in this globe of destruction...

My friend, seek to know how to help thy afflicted fellow creatures. I have observed your constancy and attention. If You will be my disciple or scholar, signify the same by letter and I will try thee whether thou art fit - and if so I will initiate thee into the highest mysteries of the discipline.

I would advise you that all worldliness must be done away with and neither family nor friends nor foes nor any other consideration must amuse you from your duty which is principally the true adoration of the most high God and to study how to do your duty in this Vale of Misery - both towards God and your neighbours.

These things being premised when you use the Crystal see that you touch no animal food for 24 hours nor drink no strong liquors whatever 'till the going down of the Sun and then only sufficient to clear nature and refresh the body.

Meditate day and night on what you desire to know, have ready pen and ink perfumes-the virgin parchment - 2 wax candles and 2 clean candle sticks and a small earthen dish with lighted charcoal, likewise the Pentacle of Solomon which you ought to draw out as described in the Magus (here is meant a hexagon, a Star of David) upon a piece of virgin parchment, likewise the name Tetragrammaton - (YHVH)- written upon a piece of vellum fastened around your forehead like a wreath. (spotless white vellum will do instead of virgin parchment , and for Tetragrammaton write, simply, YHVH -author - and for the Pentacle of Solomon substitute the sign of the Hexagram - Star of David - drawn out in black on a silver plate).

Have ready a new phial filled with clear oil - Olive, with which you must anoint your eyelids and the palms of both hands. Let the Crystal be placed between the two candles, but first of all it must be consecrated. (To consecrate is easy -just lay your hands on each object, call upon your Higher Self and breathe gently upon each object, saying each time: "it is done, so let it be!" -author).

When all is ready walk three times clockwise around the room, saying three times: "In the Name of the most high God let nothing untoward enter this my sanctuary upon pain of total obliteration by the most High Lord now guarding this most sacred temple which is now in the realm of our ancient ones, so let it be!"

*The operation now begins.

"In the name of the most high God I conjure thee thou spirit (name the spirit -) by the power of the Supreme Creator to appear here to me in this Crystal that thou shalt give me true answers concerning these things I desire to know and to be informed of and truly to instruct and to show us our desire without any guile or craft, this I conjure thee quickly to do in the name of the Great Work, so let it be .. .

"Also I do conjure thee by the Land, by the Trees, by the Sea, by the Shore, by the Stars and by the Stones, by the Earth and all things above and below the Earth, by the Thunder and the Lightning and by all the elements that thou spirit whom I invoke do quickly appear in this Crystal visibly and with a plain and intelligible voice show me those things which are proven for me to know, and answer and inform me of these things, so let it be!"

(The spirit will appear after having read the Call fervently on thy knees 7 times over).

Then being satisfied of what thou wouldst know of the spirit use this dismissal or licence for the spirit to depart which thou shalt not detain above one quarter of an hour.

The License

God hath appointed thee a place, go in His Name to wherever thou art familiar. Be ready to come when I call thee in His Name to whom every knee doth bow of things
in Heaven and things on Earth and things under the Earth, I license thee to depart, so let it be!"
(Here return thanks to God with any prayers thou mayest think proper).

Note

Before you intend to work, observe to be clean washed and linen clean in your clothing. Also let there be a new clean linen on the table under the Crystal.

Let your incense be strong and plenty of it, and let all things be consecrated by you and bless the water with salt.

This is the end of Barrett's Instruction Manuscript for the practical operation. I have kept the quaint 18th century English and tidied up the punctuation etc without taking in any away from the Mss. Barrett immediately follows on this powerful practical ritual with an essay titled On Spiritual Vision, which was obviously considered by the Magus to be of the utmost importance to those who sought to be his disciples. Today's Druids, our students and others interested in the Path of the Magus will find its theoretical and practical implications to be of real value.

ON SPIRITUAL VISION

The ancient Magi, amongst their philosophical researches into nature and magic, discovered a possibility of communicating with celestial and astral spirits, that is by fasting and prayer they received oracles from God, though the medium of the celestial spirits who received their instructions from the Blessed Intelligences or Seven Spirits who constantly stand before the face of God. By these means they drew as it were from the original Archetype of all things the knowledge of future events and the prediction of the contingencies of human affairs. Not only in the knowledge of nature and natural things, but likewise they discovered further that the four elements had their invisible as well as their visible inhabitants from the highest to the lowest, i.e. from the heavens to the earth. Therefore they divided those legions into sundry classes. First they set in order the Nine Quires of Angels, then followed with the spirits of the fiery regions, then of the airy regions, of the watery, and finally of the earthly of the Earth, which were not properly to be called astral spirits, as these were more nearly assimilated to the nature of man and were found even to be subject to human affections and to solicit a kind of copulation with men and women.

These different orders of spirits, astral, elementary etc. are fully described in my book The Magus, therefore it is needless to be repeated here. My intent is to come directly to the forms and the ways by which the wise ancients attracted those spirits into communication, which was accounted by them and all others no trifling or easy operation, but the highest point of human wisdom, to which they gave the title Magic, a name sufficient enough for such a scope of knowledge as enabled men to know and converse not only with visible creatures, but with invisible angels and spirits. This they did by various forms, prayers, invocations, suffumigations, mirrors, glasses, circles and the like attended with abstinence from carnal affairs and perturbations of the mind. But one method that was held in great repute was a mode of invoking spirits by a crystal, of which I intend to speak principally in this place.

But first it is necessary for me to explain to you that they made use of these four instruments in the invocation of spirits:

First you must consider that it is the law, in natural as well as in occult philosophy, that no spirit, seeing that they are of an immaterial form, can manifest themselves to the human eye without some medium by which they can somehow materialise their spiritual and immortal bodies, nor can flesh and blood see but what is in some sort substantial, and of its own nature, for we cannot see fire without some material body as wood, flint, steel etc., nor can we see the air unless it is coloured, although we perceive it both hot and cold, yet still it remains invisible to sight, smell or touch unless it be moved or stirred up or perfumed or coloured. Therefore, seeing that the nature and operations of spirits are so very different to those of tangible bodies, hence arose the great difficulty of a spirit manifesting itself to the human organs, without some medium being used by him who would communicate with them. But it was discovered that this inconvenience was in a great measure removed by using some certain things agreeable and sympathising with the nature of the spirits. Nothing was found more adapted than powerful suffumigations. By the thick vapour and clouds produced by these, it not only enabled the spirits to clothe themselves with an artificial and temporary body producing a certain visible appearance to the human sight. These suffumigations and these perfumes served a twofold purpose, first to render the operation more attractive as well as to spiritualise the operator, and excite his spirit, and make him more fit for such an operation, he having previously prepared by long fasting and abstinence from every gross and superfluous thing relative to the flesh.

For it is undoubtedly held by all who know anything of spiritual operations, that at the time and minute of a spirit's becoming visible it is such a shock to our frail natural body that a sickness and a trembling fall upon man, almost like to death, and by an indispensable law of providence he is rapt up as it were in a delirious ecstasy of soul , and it requires every resolution, faith and firmness of soul, to stand firmly before such tremendous visitors. I am speaking chiefly of the operation by a circle.

The other method of communicating which is by a Crystal or a smooth shining steel mirror is not attended by such a violent conflict of soul and body - although I deem a suffumigations in necessary in this as the other, and this brings me to the subject on which you desire me to speak, which I will here set down everything that is needed to be done for the obtaining of a spiritual vision in a Crystal, which you may try whenever convenient. First I would advise you that all perfumes, papers, pentacles, times, hours, even the Crystal itself, will not be of any use whatsoever, unless you can entirely abstract your mind from every worldly affair for a season, excite within yourself the supernatural powers, and firmly ground within yourself a strong and vehement faith (which is the chief key of this art). For seven days at least fast and abstain from all heavy rich and strong drink, and take nothing from the rising to the going down of the Sun except bread and water (preferably water from the well). After sunset you may without inconvenience take some simple and light refreshments. Every morning pray for what you desire in a quiet place free from noise and bustle. Without these observations nothing can be done either by Crystal or circle.

Do not touch the Crystal with your hands after placing it on the table. Have ready some clean white paper to write down the name of the spirit, his planet sign and character which he may show you.

Afterwards put what questions you may wish to be informed of, returning thanks to the Creator. Ask the spirit at what seasons and times it would be most eligible and agreeable for him to come to you, and for what business

his character is proper to be used for, and on what occasions.
Ask him all those things which seem agreeable to his nature and his office to communicate.
When all this is done, and a quarter of an hour expired, license him to depart and return thanks to God.

These things being duly observed I think you are a man permitted, or designed to work in these mysteries, that you will not fail of the desired success, with which I beg leave to conclude this present writing and am Sir

Your Friend etc., F.B. May 51 1802

Chapter Seventeen

The Celtic Tree Oracle

The beauty and the power of the Druid's art is unleashed in the casting of the Ogham sticks in divination.

The Ogham alphabet goes back as far as 200 A.D. This final artistic flourish of the Druids lasted right across the centuries into our own time.

Ogham casting is as effective as the tarot and the runes. Divination is by use of the alphabet of the Druids. The twenty letters of Ogham are all named after trees. Each tree in the Tree Alphabet has a set of meanings and correspondences attached to it, and all the tree letters are linked to themes and figures from Celtic mythology. Each has its own distinct wisdom. In divination these letters interact with a person's own special circumstances.

Traditionally Ogham letters were carved on staves of yew. In The Wooing of Etain we read, "at last a Druid named Dallan learned, by means of Oghams carved on wands of yew, that she was hidden under Midir's sidh." Here we see an actual Druid practice Ogham divination more powerfully than any tarot!

There are twenty basic letters of Ogham that are formed by cutting notches or strokes across a central line or bar. Five extra letters were added later on. The main branch of Ogham has letters named after trees and it is the rough ancestor of the alphabet of the ancient Irish language. In another version of the tale of Midir and Etain, "Codal of the Withered Breast took four rods of yew and wrote Oghams on them and through his enchantments he found that Etain was with Mider in Bri Leith."

This is indeed the most powerful magic and you can try it for yourself. Even better, you can cut your own set of Ogham rods.

The Ogham Tract, a key medieval document on Ogham, tells us:

Whence is the origin of Ogham? Not hard. I shall speak firstly of the woods of the trees whence names have been put to the Ogham letters ...it is from the trees of the forest that names were given to the Ogham letters metaphorically. "
The Beth Luis Nian Tree Alphabet, called after the first three letters in the alphabet, is the ·main one used in divination today. The Ogham Tract continues:

What are the place, time, person and the cause of the invention of the Ogham? Not hard. Its place the island of Ireland where the Irish live. Now Ogma, a man well skilled in speech and in poetry invented the Ogham. The cause of its invention, as a matter of proof of his ingenuity, and that this speech should belong to the learned apart, to the exclusion of rustics and herdsmen ... "

Why trees? Why are trees thought in the Celtic mind to possess the best properties for magical and divinatory purposes? Because the trees of the greenwood are the divine energies upon the earth and they are also our neighbours here, watching us come and go.

Indeed our roots are holy. .
Druidry does not necessarily follow a pagan path, rather it can follow the path of any religion on God's earth and there is little to prevent it merging with forms of Christianity. Indeed it has done so on several occasions in the past. In Ireland today it finds itself practiced as part of the Christianity of Father Daragh Molloy on the Aran Islands and as a smaller part of the poetic writings of John O'Donoghue. It is no less authentic for all of that.

Colin and Liz Murray made the first effort in reviving Ogham as a popular oracle in 1988 when The Celtic Tree Oracle: a system of divination was published. This was an important breakthrough by Colin, who died prematurely around that time, and who was one of the principal revivers of Druidry in the latter half of the twentieth century.

Known by his Druidic name, Coll Hazel Wand he was Chief of the Golden Section Order which based its ritual on the Golden Dawn ceremonial. He was the archetypical scholarly middle-class English occult type, like Ronald Hutton who followed him, who fashioned large Druidic Orders based on an eclectic mixture of esoterica and wrote relatively harmless books of a.high literary standard about Druidry. Their writing is exquisite, the best since the romantic writers of the eighteenth century.

Since Colin's death Liz Murray has been outstanding as organiser, secretary, liaison officer and general peacemaker on behalf of the Council of British Druid Orders, which is now broadly recognised as the leading Druid Council in the world. (The present author is an Honoured Associate of the Council).

Colin and Liz Murray followed Robert Graves' idea of the Tree calendar, but their primary focus is on practical divination. They state that, "the use of this alphabet is symbolic and...each letter has a host of ideas and thoughts centered around it relating to Celtic cosmology and philosophy. Seeing the Oghams as "keys that open a door to a parallel world of knowledge, meanings and associations", Colin and Liz presented their Celtic Tree Oracle as a set of cards in a wooden box with a green cloth segmented for the purpose of divination. Their commentaries on each card give its mythological meaning along with a description of each tree and set of divinatory meanings. This is still the best seller although getting increasingly hard to find in the shops in these modern times. All the chiefs, and most of the Indians too, of all the Druid Orders, have their sets.

If you can't readily find a set to purchase, contact the Council of British Druid Orders, 76 Antrobus Road, Chiswick, London W4. This is the very best contact address of all in the world today for all matters druidic.

THE VISION AND THE VOICE

The blackness gathers about, so thick, so clinging, so penetrating, so oppressive, that all the other darknesses that I have ever conceived would be like bright light beside it.

His voice comes in a whisper: "O thou that art master of the gates of understanding, O thou that art master of the silver pentagram, is not the egg of spirit the Druid egg?

Here abides terror and the blind ache of the soul."

"I am the sightless storm in the night that wraps the world about with desolation. Chaos is my name, and thick darkness. Know thou that the darkness of the earth is brown, the darkness of the air is grey, but the darkness of the soul is utter blackness."

"The white stones of the Druid are crowned with golden flame."

And I was about to answer him: "The light is within me". But before I could frame the words, he answered me with the great word that is the key of the abyss. And he said: "Thou hast entered night, dust thou yet lust for day?" Sorrow is my name and affliction. I am girt about with tribulation. Here the mother weeps over the children that she hath not borne. Sterility is my name and desolation. Intolerable is thine ache and incurable thy wound."

What I thought were shapes of rocks, rather felt than seen, now appear to be veiled bishops sitting absolutely still and silent. Nor can one be distinguished from the others.

And the Angel sayeth: "Behold where thine Angel has led thee. Thou didst ask for fame, power and pleasure, health and wealth and love, and strength and length of days. Thou didst hold life with eight tentacles, like an octopus. Thou didst seek the four powers and the seven delights and the twelve emancipations and the two and twenty privileges and the nine and forty manifestations, and lo! Thou art become as one of these. Bowed are their backs, whereon rests the universe. Veiled are their faces that have beheld the glory Ineffable."

And the Angel sayeth: "Verily is the cathedral a temple. Verily also is it a tomb. Thinkest thou that there is life in the Bishops of the Temple that sit hooded, encamped upon the sea of daath. Verily there is no life in them. And the beatific vision is no more, and the glory of the Most High is no more. There is no more knowledge. There is no more bliss. There is no more power. There is no more beauty. For this is the Palace of Understanding."

"Drink in the myrrh of my speech. For as pure being is pure nothing, so is pure wisdom pure folly, and so is pure understanding silence, stillness and darkness."

"I am sent from the Father to expound all things discreetly in these the last words that thou shalt here before thou take thy seat among these bishops whose eyes are sealed up, and whose ears are stopped, and whose mouths are clenched, who are folded in upon themselves, the red liquor of whose bodies is dried up, so that nothing remains but grey cathedrals of dust."

"And that bright light of comfort, and that piercing sword of truth, and all that power and beauty that they have made of themselves, is cast from them, as it is written "like lightning from the heavens".

And I cried out: "For the trouble with them is that they wished to substitute the blood of someone else for their own blood, because they wanted to keep their own personalities forever here on high."

A voice crashed through the heavens: "Verily I hear the voice of a wise one!"

And like a speeding flame the sword of truth drops through the abyss, where the four beasts keep watch. And it appears in the heavens as a morning or an evening star. And the silver light thereof shines even unto the Earth, and brings hope and help to them that dwell in the darkness of thought, and drink of the poison of life, and the name of every season is death.

And so, in reward for my crying out the words of the wise, I enter the Earth once more.

And there is a blue-veiled figure in a garden. Upon the root of one flower she pours acid so that the root writhes as if in torture. And another she cuts and it shrieks like a mandrake torn up by the roots. Another she sears with fire.

The last flower she lovingly anoints with holy oil.

And I greet:"Heavy is the labour, but great indeed the reward." She an-

swered: "I shall not see the reward, I only tend the garden." And I asked: "What of the three murdered flowers?"
And she answered: "There was only enough brown earth to keep but one good flower for your new incarnation."

And I asked: "What flower is it?"
So sweet she smiled as she replied:
"It is the flower of wisdom"

The Metaphysics of Druidry

Chapter Eighteen

In our own Rite

There are delicate reasons why popular Druid writers deliberately avoid the question - Is Druidry a religion? Some of them are chiefs of Druid Orders and we have people coming in, starting out or rather faltering along the first steps of the path of the Druid, people who have spent half a lifetime in some religion or church or other, usually Christian. Such people want to be helped along easily. There is some mind baggage to be left behind. There are many reasons we ourselves manufacture to avoid reaching any conclusion on whether Druidry is a religion or not. Most people are very wary of committing themselves publicly to a certain position: "What if I am wrong?" That awful word 'failure' is something we have drummed into us from an early age as something to be avoided at all cost. So we hold on tightly to doctrines and dogma which we know to be false and to have failed us, when it is so easy to let go lightly.

The biggest failure is death and we all fail that way. The truth can be hard to face and even harder to act upon. So if you wish to conclude that Druidry is not a religion, what then is it? A way of life? Certainly. spirituality... We druids are all on this journey together in which a whole new spirit evolves, step by step, leap by leap. We are voracious. Our appetite for knowledge and wisdom overcomes every other spirituality, every religion, as we accelerate, leaving the old-fashioned, the clingers to outmoded beliefs, the begrudgers, and the simply lazy, behind. We have solved mysteries. There are more ahead. This is why we simply must explore the furthest reaches of the magical and the mystical. We have passed into realms where no religion, no church, no religion has gone before. Indeed we have bypassed our ancestral Druids with the aid of modern science. We have made real discoveries and we hold on to them fiercely.

So, to pose the question again - Is Druidry a religion? As you can see it is far more than that. There are those who hold that the question cannot be answered, because such a question delves into the heart of the mysteries. Ah what are Druids but solvers of mysteries! To answer the question even more explicitly we have to ask two more questions: "What is religion?" and "What is Druidry?" Religion and Druidry are both parts of the mysteries and as such are extremely difficult to convey to others in words, especially written words in which language is inadequate. But Druids never give up trying to explain to people.

THE SIX DIMENSIONS

Here I consider religion as opposed to religions, an abstract rather than actual and particular system of religious beliefs. Druidry is not and never was and hopefully never will be a church. To understand Druidry you must realise that it was there long before the concept of church in the modern sense was ever even dreamt of, so it cannot possibly be looked upon in such modern terms as church or denomination. For it was among the original belief systems of the world. Religion is an organism of many dimensions typically encompassing doctrines, myths, ethical teachings, rituals and social institutions. Straightaway Druidry does not qualify as a religion, far less a church, under one of these headings, doctrine. For Druidry has no doctrine. But, has it? Be careful.

Druidry has recently begun to develop doctrines - that the supreme deity is/was a goddess, for instance, that religion must not be patriarchal, that it must be matriarchal, that all other beliefs outside of Druidry, and outside the beliefs held by the present leaders of Druidry, are wrong - here we have nothing less than creeping infallibility! Thankfully none of this has got a grip in Ireland. Not yet.

In his book The Religious Experiences of Man Ninian Smart goes on to suggest that there are six essential dimensions to the religious organism. These are the ritual (sacred and pragmatic), mythological, doctrinal, ethical, social and experiential dimensions. To these might be added the charismatic, the historical/traditional and the artistic, and Druidry has all three of these in abundance.

Ritual has two aspects: sacred ritual which refers to actions, ceremonies, objects, art forms, music, chants and so on which are given or have sacred significance. Druidry has all these on a par with any religion. Then there is the pragmatic ritual which refers to self-development, not necessarily acts of worship or devotion to a particular deity. Then Druidry has the additional historic technique of understanding the cosmos through science. This distinguishes it from all extant religions.

The doctrinal dimension does not exist formally in Druidry, although I warn that it is fast creeping in. Doctrine becomes dogma, beliefs that members have to accept. There are, in English Druidry now, rules that all adherents

must obey, leaders that all adherents must obey if they want to progress! None of this applies in Ireland. Not yet!
The ethical dimension refers to concepts of good moral behaviour in particular and in this Druidry scores as well as any extant religion in today's world.

The social dimension, which bonds people together in communities, is evident in Druidry In most Druid Orders today there is a certain hierarchy but it is either elected or based on broad consensus.

Apart from this Druids do not seem to want to know about organisation, structure and institution when it comes to the Orders of which they are members.

Druidry possesses, more powerfully I would argue, the experiential dimension, than any-religion. It searches and probes into realms where no religion or church dare go. It probes that which lies at the very heart of religion.

Now, is Druidry a religion? It is not because it does not have to be. It is because it is all that spirit desires. And it is more. The first steps across the abyss, which separate us from perfection, are those from mere faith to knowledge, from doubtful belief to certainty, from knowledge and certainty to experience of the mysteries and wisdom. These steps are not necessary for the 'Faithfull' masses of the churches and the religions - mass mesmerism and continuous reinforcement at church ceremonies suffice there. Faith is sufficient as a crutch to the uninitiated, as a consolation in times of desolation, and is difficult only insofar as it requires a sustained effort on behalf of the Faith-full. Faith can be twisted and the Faith-full misled.

Knowledge removes the Wise One from that. From the ranks of the Faith-full are recruited the armies of the religions and the churches.
From the ranks of the Knowing nobody is recruited, and as the Knowing has always been and still is a small minority, Druidry has not, nor does it now, seek armies.

In the religions and churches you practice what you are programmed from childhood to believe, and you believe what you practice into old age.

You can always fall back on the charismatic dimension. If you belong to a church/religion that claims its powers derive from the miraculous life and work of a person who is usually held in divine awe, you become 'born again' in the image of that particular divine person, assuming the attraction, inspiration, example and finally the authority of that historic person. You can then go forth and bring others to this blissful stage of being 'born again' and thus reinforce your ego rather than tend to your spirit/soul.

Then there is the art of religion. Again, the only 'religion' to powerfully infuse scientific codes and ciphers into their art were the Druids, their 'rock art' being equivalent to megalithic computer print-outs. And, as we saw, they encoded much of their mathematical, astronomical and calendrical knowledge in addition to Newgrange and Stonehenge. This flowered into the Druidic art used in magnificent decoration of the early Irish manuscripts.

The Celto-Druidic art was pressed into service by the early monks and given a new and lasting outlet in these the most richly and artistically decorated books the world has ever seen.

For all of this, the single most important aspect of religion is the experiential. There are those who consider it to be the only one. And this leads to our second question of "What is Druidry?"

Druids were the intellectuals of Celtic society. They were the philosophers, the judges, the doctors and healers, the historians, the poets and literati, the astronomers, the prophets, priests and kings. They were peacemakers and diplomats. In war they formed the general staffs of the Celtic armies Above all they were the glue that held the..Celtic tribes and nations together. They had grades of Bard, Ovate and Druid, in Ireland of File, Faith and Drui, which are loosely equivalent today to the university degrees of Bachelor, Master and Doctor. Indeed the Irish Fili had the top grade of Ard Ollamh which translates directly into English as High Professor.

They founded and presided over the forerunners of the universities throughout the British Isles and France. They had groves at Oxford and twenty-one other sites on which today's universities sit.

Here I hasten to add that we have nothing in common with a system which grants 'intellectualism' to the materially rich. The present university system actively discriminates against many people of high intelligence who do not have the money to pay for the degrees - shades of paying for indulgences that led to the Protestant Reformation. The system of formal education at

the higher levels in our society is gross perversion, based more on bank balance than the balance of intelligence.
Access to university degrees encourages pseudo-intellectual snobbery and despises genius.

The higher degrees are the preserve of a wealthy elite while intellect, like almost everything else of value in our world, is trampled on.   · The Druids had a well-defined legal system called the Brehon Laws, This code has never been abolished in Ireland to this day. Marriages under the Brehon Laws are recognised to this day bJLfhe State-in Ireland. Today we sit in judgment on the status quo. How we judge and act on these judgements has an effect on the world as we cast our pebbles into the pond and the ripples radiate.

So when Druidry is compared with the dimensions of religion it is easy to see that there are correspondences, direct and indirect. But nothing corresponds exactly. It seems that Druidry has more. Religion is a self-absorbed thing for self-absorbed people. It is rigidly defined and fenced in. Druidry, which is free spirit, could never be that.

So where does this leave you if you don't want religion? If you do not embrace religion, if you do not believe in deities, you can still be a Druid. For in ancient times all priests were Druids but not all Druids were priests.

As a Druid I work to know and to preserve the history of our way and our people; to know and protect the places of our way; to express the way in all its forms through arts, crafts, and all the actions of my life; to keep alive the traditions of our way; to seek out and preserve the ancient wisdom; to uphold the freedom to right expression; to learn and understand and keep the sacred word; to open doors with the power of the word; to be a force for good in the world.

I work to know and understand and respect nature, her creature peoples and their ways; know compassion, and, in accordance with my skills, heal the hurts of the world; converse with our ancestors; explore and come to know the Otherworld; understand the mysteries of death and rebirth; cultivate intuition; open the doors of time and there travel freely.

I work to achieve authority in ritual and ceremonial; understand and keep right law; offer good counsel and advice; investigate and understand the cosmos.

It is from the practical application of this work, my understanding of my place in the world and the journey I have undertaken, that I derive what follows. For, just as we can describe religion in terms of the dimensions it consists of, so we can define Druidry. However, where religion is seen as having six dimensions, Druidry to me consists of nine.

THE NINE WAVES OF DRUIDRY

The first of these I call the national dimension, as it is that which encompasses the language, history, traditions, mythology, wisdom, and geography of the people - everything that has to do with the identity of the nation and its relation to both time and space.

Then there is the dimension of craft, which has to do with the broadest sense of the word running from what we now call arts and handicrafts to permaculture, earth energies and crystal workings.

Next is the dimension of healing, for which is needed an understanding of the world and all that is in it, of the ways in which the Earth and her children come to be damaged, and of the ways in which each of us can best use our own skills to aid in their (and so our own) salvation.

The metaphysical dimension is concerned primarily with the mysteries of being, of life, death and rebirth, and of the understanding of these and other things that can be distilled from contact with our ancestors and exploration of the Otherworld.

Complementing the metaphysical, which draws a great deal on the past is the dimension of divination in which the developed forces of the intuition are let range across those parts of the great wheel of time that move towards us and in which we learn to understand what we might glimpse of that which may come to be.

The dimension of natural philosophy is the search for understanding of the ways and war.kings of the world and the universe, primarily that of cosmology.

The ritual dimension is that which unfolds the rituals and ceremonials of Druidry, primarily the festivals of the year.

There is the dimension of magic - the path of high Druidry.

Finally there is the dimension of service.

Druidry is about working to place the truth against the world so as to make it a better place for all. All that we become as Druids is there for all others. There is one further distinction that will help to clarify the position. In 1913 the Swedish scholar Nathan Soderblom noted a distinction that is embraced by most of the world's great religions.

He wrote: Holiness is the great word of religion; it is even more essential than the notion of God. Real religion may exist without a definitive concept of the divinity, but there is no real religion without a distinction between the holy and the profane.

Two words here need quick consideration, for both have a number of meanings. Holy means sacred, pertaining to deity, held in religious awe, saintly, free from sin, pious, connected with religion. Profane means showing contempt for sacred things or persons, blasphemous, not concerned with sacred matters, secular, not initiated, ignorant of sacred things, wicked.

By that distinction Druidry is not a real religion because Druidry does not recognise that there can be anything in the world but the sacred. All things are sacred. .All things are truth. The thoughts and actions of human beings are another matter for they are, in the main, inventions, that is, re-arrangements of already ordered things. These rearrangements can act in concord with the world or they can be in discord.

Druidry contains within it all the requisites to become a religion if it wants to, but that does not bound it. We do not want to stop at being a religion for Druidry has never in its history wanted to stop at that. When you stop you stagnate. You never discover anything new. When you stop you have nothing that is really yours to pass on. We must therefore continue to discuss all things carefully and extensively, knowing that we are moving closer to the ultimate answer.

Chapter Nineteen

The Graceful Druid

"I strove with none for none were worth my strife, Nature I loved and next to nature, Art: I warmed both hands before the fire of life; It sinks, and I am ready to depart."

Walter Savage Landor (1775-1864)

The sunset was a great red glow speared through with shafts of silvered gold. The Druidic Trinity of the sea and the sky and the land fused together and the sun ran an amber stream between them.

I strolled across to the edge of the cliff as my spirit stretched between the land and the sea and the sky. The sun slowly slid down and sent rays of peace into my soul.

Maybe the sunset is one of the faces of God.

To be Druid, working publicly in, say, Chelsea or Rathmines, is a task I would enjoy. For the world looks kindly on Druids in such liberal climes. To be Druid walking in the world is still not an easy path to tread. Several Druids I know are 'in the closet' in the more rural parts of these isles, as they are in the American Deep South. Still it is not as dangerous as being Jew in Tehran. Yet for us to walk in the world requires great wisdom and knowledge of a good many things. Most of these things are familiar to us since being drawn to the path of the Druid is a gradual and learning process.

Once on the path we learn anew and come to understand more fully ways that were formerly hidden to us. In this way we re-explore the charted and venture more widely into the uncharted territories of our selves where we learn much that gives us the strength, the knowledge and the wisdom to serve. Times are much better for us today, even in the more rural backwoods. We may well lose votes or business in such provincial places, where churchman, party politician and local journal still hold sway, for being Druid, but not our limbs or our lives. Like Landor, we strive with none ...

Our universe is a vast and complex place, extremely ancient, with all prospect that it will continue to be for time out of mind. So it is a place that is very easy, even for the most astute, to get lost in. This is why a sense of place, a sense of rootedness, is so important to us in our world. The land, a centre, home - these are the heart positions from which we take our bearings on our outward journeys and which are the beacons that light and guide our return. Our inner planes, so beloved by solitaries, are not in our material incarnation the place of home - no matter how welcome any of us may be there, no matter how much we may desire it. There is no physical point there on which to centre ourselves permanently. This is why we have spirit guides to keep us oriented. And this is why, when we extend our work in the world, it is done through the medium of our ancestors and the responsibilities we have towards our descendants in time.

Coming to know and understand ourselves and our universe is not all there is to becoming a Druid, although we will have approached these tasks or quests from that perspective.

Such high knowledge or understanding of things as we gain upon the path, no matter how comprehensive and deep, lacks the energy that will give it life. Without life it will all have been an interesting task. And those who undertake it, if they take it no further than that, will always be bereft of power to make right change in the world. Making right change in the world is what service, the essence of Druidry, is all about.

So what more must be done and whence comes that vital energy? The answer is connection, with the Circle, with the Grove, with the Order, to re-energise the psychic fires across the land and throughout the world. It is the forging of links through which the primal energies of existence can flow to us and through us. Of course such energies cannot be allowed to flow unchecked or unguided for they will overwhelm and destroy us as surely as they will harm the land and the rest of the world. Therefore, in order to vitalize our knowledge and understanding, and release the power inherent in what we have learned and channel it to right service, we must come to know how we, as persons who are Druid, stand in relation to the world. And in that knowing and understanding we must become practiced in that relation, for all relations are active and dynamic, as is Druidry active and dynamic at outer world level through its Druid Orders, Circles and Groves. After all, what use is your knowledge, your understanding, your wisdom, if it does not color and guide your living and working in and with the world?

Coming to know and understand how we Druids stand in relation to the world is the most difficult of the complex quests that face us. Not only do such investigations have no place in your normal scheme of things, making them alien to your way of thought, but working with the basic elements of existence is also absent from everyday consideration.
Certain inbuilt structures, fundamental to the maintenance of mundane society and the educational system it spawns, inhibit questioning of such things. It is, therefore, not something that comes naturally to us as a field of study. Indeed we all too easily assume that our relation to the world is something that just happens, sorting itself out as we go along. As a result the establishment, maintenance and development of such relations is often neglected. Yet we cannot afford to leave such an important aspect of our being unquestioned or to develop as chance dictates, because what we are and how we relate to everything else is at the heart of Druidry. But that is not all.

In exploring our relation with the world we find that it reaches into both space and time. Space is the easier of these areas to work with. Time is an unfamiliar territory, which, like the inner planes, requires us to find guides with whom we can identify our ancestors. In establishing stronger connection with, and understanding of our relationship with our ancestors, it is all too easy to lose touch, not only with ourselves, but also with the understanding we have of what our self is. We lose touch because of the very thing we do - all the time we work and explore we are evolving and the links we have forged with the world are forever changing. What each of us is now is different from what we were when we first trod the path, even if that was but a few weeks ago.

If we lose sight of what we are constantly becoming then we lose sight of the world and the light of our being.

For in our relationship with the world and in the flow of energies back and forth between our evolving self and the rest of the world is to be found the dynamic tension of our personal existence. This it is that stimulates being, drives evolution, kindles learning, increases understanding and gives birth to joy.

Through this perspective - the dynamic tension of our existence - brought alive by our quest along the highways and byways of Druidry, we come to know and understand our selves, the world, and our place in it, as well as our pasts, our presents and our futures. The more we search, the wider and brighter are the panoramas and the horizons, the vistas we are enabled to explore.

In doing this we are also assisting others in their quest to know and understand their relation with the spatial and temporal world more clearly, because our existence , being dynamic and directed toward an influence of the primal energies, resonates positively though space and time. Not only do we live many lives but each one of those lives touches the lives of many others - most directly in whatever is our present. But there is more to it than that. We are the future to those in our past, and we are ancestors as well - ancestors to be. So it is that we have a responsibility to those that have been, our present companions, and those who will come after us (ourselves re incarnate, after all) to manage ourselves and our relationship to the world with excellence and grace.

THE GRACEFUL DRUID

Grace is now a difficult concept to come to grips with as the use of the word has become more polarised in recent centuries. In common parlance it has increasingly come to be associated solely with the outward appearance of things, especially movement. In church parlance it is used in the sense of the condition of being favoured by God, being "in a state of grace", and it is thus seen by many people as a purely spiritual phenomenon. To further complicate matters, grace is often regarded as an end in itself. This disassociation of meaning, along with the belief in grace as an end in itself, can be for the good. But it demeans true grace. Where grace is truly present it permeates the whole being. It is a divine influence operating in and through people to regenerate and sanctify the world. This can only work if grace is made manifest both physically and spiritually. Furthermore, grace is a state that enables us to influence the world and we attain it as a result of the way we interact with the world. It can only be achieved, the divine influence can only be attracted and channelled, by acting and thinking in right manner.

Now we come to the old adage - no man is an island. If you try to be an island then you are not Druid. This arises from an understanding of -where is the boundary between me and 'not me'? This question is of supreme importance for it is fundamental to the Druid Way, the way we treat the planet, whether you look upon the Earth as Gaia, or as the Great Mother, or even as a goddess, or none of these.

If, in asking myself, I answer that myself is the border beyond which the rest of the world begins, I immediately alienate myself from everything else that exists. Stating this, I cannot thereafter truly claim to know anything about the world with certainty. The world becomes wholly other. It becomes physically, aesthetically, spiritually, intellectually, emotionally and politically unknowable, untouchable and closed to influence by me.

I could not even logically talk about 'us' because I could only know and acknowledge existence of my self with any certainty. And in the end, not even that old sa\v cogito ergo sum is tautological. Thus isolated, my vision of my self becomes, of necessity, synchronous and synonymous with my physical body. That becomes my central concern. The spirit withers. I become truly selfish.

Anybody adopting this model of the self (and many do) will suffer great psychic and psychological distress simply because it is an untenable position -no matter how much they may pretend otherwise. They cannot rely on the Cartesian tautology to demonstrate, assert and maintain their being. They cannot stand in splendid isolation. This is because the self has to have interaction with the rest of the world if only to survive - air, water, food, people and so on - let alone flourish. Without it, psychoses set in and begin to govern both thought and action. This may seem to beg the question of whether or not the world is an objective reality existing independently of our perception of it. It matters not.

Real in that sense or not, the rest of the world is essential to self-being no matter how much that may be denied. Here we have a fundamental difference between the philosophy of the western Druidic Wisdom Tradition and that of the various religions of india and the Far East that view the world as an illusion.

The problem is that such a view of the world as Buddhism for instance, quite apart from psychotic thought and behaviour of some of the other eastern offshoots that treats the world as wholly other or as illusion, locks the people that genuinely hold . such views into vicious circles. Their denial of the world causes them distress. And distress will often manifest itself as denial. Yet the world is there and it will not ignore a person no matter how much they try to ignore it. The more the world tries to break through into their isolation the more such people, including those involved in the more fearsome Christian-based fundamentalist cults such as we have seen at Jonestown and Waco, as well as the more terrifying Islamic cults of Al Qaeda, react aggressively and attempt, under the influence of some charismatic leader like Asama Bin Laden, or some other guru or 'prophet-figure', to destroy the world that is so embarrassing to them and to their beliefs. That destruction can be of the world - and of the self. It can be aided by so-called 'cult-busters' who go around like bounty hunters taking the law into their own hands - the terrorists of the spiritual world who are usually uneducated, very ignorant and highly dangerous.

If you walk in a forest all that you experience there shapes you. While you are there the forest is physically, aesthetically, spiritually, emotionally and intellectually part of yourself, just as your self is part of the forest. And even as you leave the forest it remains part of your self and you remain part of it. For it will have changed you as you changed it. Our self moves through life expanding and touching in a vital dance of the essential self, living its own existence, distinct from but never separate from all existences. We are all part of one another, part of every creature, every star, flower and stone, part of all that is, that was and that will ever be.

This awesome Druidic and beautiful way of looking at the world and living in it and through all worlds has many responsibilities that are closer to home. Harm any part of the world and sooner or later we harm ourselves. We cannot avoid changing the world as we pass through, performing our function of living.

Chapter Twenty

The Truth against the World

The Truth against the World - that famous Druidic motto - is a contentious phrase. It is one that deserves our closest consideration, especially among Druids, because meditation upon its meaning reaches to the heart of our being, what we are, what we do, the way we live our lives on both our inner and outer planes.

One of the questions often asked of adherents of religions, faiths or churches (and especially of mystery traditions like Druidry) is - Why? Why Christianity? Why Islam? Why Buddhism/ Why Druidry? Of course the question has much to do with where you were born. In these islands of Britain and Ireland, and in North America, Australasia etc. we have to a great extent a choice concerning what spiritual path we tread. Although England, for instance, has always been a Christian country, this is now little more than a political facade. The old ways are still strong and there is a relatively free choice in how people decide to express themselves spiritually. If you were born, however, in Belfast, Tehran or Salt Lake City, your path is chosen and it takes a particular kind of courage and strength to break away from the path presented as the 'true' or the 'only' one and choose another. And I do absolutely mean courage, bravery of the highest.

This may not seem relevant to the questions we here address, but it is. No matter how much we may discuss matters and come to conclusions, such disputation is of little use if the results are not applicable to our everyday lives and to our spiritual quest. This is one reason why philosophy has become so devalued over the past couple of centuries. It has become, like the Law, so concerned with semantics that it has lost sight of the concerns of everyday life and has recently failed to keep abreast of scientific discoveries and medical advances and to explain their significance.

Let.us therefore step back to our first purpose, which is to consider what we might mean by placing the Truth against the World. An Firinne in aghaidh an Domhain - the Truth against the World: the first extant expression of this saying is to be found in one of the versions of the Audacht Morainn (The Will of Morann MacCairbre, a first century Druid Brehon). It is a curious and even quaint phrase worthy even of inclusion in, say, The Sermon on the Mount. Certainly its ambiguities make it difficult to comprehend in one sense, but this very quality makes it an excellent teaching device. Remember, our ancient Druids spoke in riddles so that only those most dedicated to learning could really understand. So in trying to unravel its various shades of meaning we have to investigate ideas and concepts of meaning that might otherwise be passed over. Moreover, no one interpretation will provide a definitive explication.

We must bring our own experience, thoughts, traditions and our years of hard study to its elucidation.

It therefore stands for all time as a means of helping us look at the Truth, the World, and how these have stood, and stand, in relation to each other across the aeons, particularly today when Fact, the Law and Justice can actually conflict and be at such odds, one with another. There is too a Druidic defiance about it.

THE BRIGHT HEART OF TRUTH

Truth does not lend itself to comprehensive definition. The more complex any attempt at a definition of Truth, just like Justice or any other such concept, becomes, the further it gets away from one. Truth has to be felt in the heart as much as understood in the head. Truth is always relative - it depends upon the culture in which it is held. One of the big problems with Truth is that it can all too often be connected solely with language. In our society it has become all too prevalent to believe the printed word, bedevilled by the world of public relations and multi-media advertising campaigns. In our world today Truth is really about language. Can you be innocent in Irish and guilty in English? So Truth cannot be limited to language, which is itself but a small part of the realm of Truth. Nor does Truth belong to the big media battalions and the big political parties, as they bombard us night and day from the mass hypnotiser in the corner of the living room. Truth belongs to the much wider world of our Being. It applies to our thoughts, words, deeds, behaviour, actions, and even more. Above all Truth applies to our ideals and actions in the bright heart of our Druid souls where the Spirit burns brighter than ten thousand suns.

It only takes common sense to realise that language is a very limited and indeed ill suited medium to express Truth. Not only, as you realise when you listen to lawyers in court and politicians in parliament, is it so very easy to utilise language to create plausible falsehoods, but language is also a medium that deals with only a small part of human experience. Any follower of the Druidic Mystery Tradition will only be well aware of that. If we confine our discussion and understanding of Truth solely to language then we confine ourselves to a tyrannical system that does not reflect the bright world. Language is a narrow-valued medium used to convey information about a multi-valued world. Too much emphasis on language can mean less of the Truth. Language is a black-and-white photograph trying to convey a multi-coloured world. It simply cannot be done. White man may not speak with forked tongue but his language may do so. Even of Druidry only one quarter of instruction can be carried out in writing, one quarter in oral language, one quarter in practice and the rest by experience of the World of Spirit.

This is why it is important for those of us who claim to be Druid to get out into the Grove and up upon the Mound, along by the riverbank and through the forest, down by holy well and alone in sacred dell, high up upon the mountain ridge and down below in the glen.

This is not because the printed word, the book, the computer or communication with people is necessarily bad - they can be extremely good, especially for those setting out along the path. It is simply that we must get things into perspective and get them right. All of this is highly important, working in the ancient sites, observing the festivals of the eightfold year, and at the right times too. Any Druid Order that concentrates simply upon issuing written correspondence courses, and doing little else, may be regarded as an academy or a college. The Druidic home study course is no substitute whatsoever for the real thing. It may be a business. It is not Druidry. And it can never convey the Truth of our ancient wisdom tradition.

We must consider Truth in a much wider perspective. A reconsideration is highly necessary at this important juncture in Druidic evolution. Truth itself has to apply to and derive from all things, taking on many extra dimensions which take it out of the narrow confines of mere language onto a higher plane that applies to the rightness and fitness of "all things bright and beautiful, all creatures great and small" in ways that are made manifest to the world for those who have ears to hear and eyes to see.

Falsehood can then be recognised in its many mazes and hidden dangers. It is very easy to wander around the Druid forest, aimlessly, and to emerge having seen or heard nothing at all. After gathering the flowers of the forest, if we wish to see the true light of the Sun, if we wish to teach unto others something of what we have learned, if we seek upon emerging to serve the outer as well as the inner planes, we must be careful where we go.

In stating that Truth in its widest sense has much to do with the rightness and fitness of things, I am not simply putting forward some new-fangled notion such as we see modern cultists, like scientologists, spring on the unwary. I am stating the belief of our ancestors that all things are connected, part of the whole. To our ancient Druids this was the natural order of things in which Truth was the preserving shrine. They did not separate spirit, politics, culture, this world, the Otherworld, although they recognised fully the differences between them, all these things that we separate out into faculties, professions and bureaucratic pigeonholes today. Nor did they separate their thoughts, words and deeds, their temporal and spiritual being, nor the world from the universe, nor star from stone, although they well understood the differences between all things. But these were all one to our ancestral Druids, each part of the whole, and each and every one investing and complementing each other in a unity of energy across the Land. Many of the problems we face today arise, in great part, from our continual and frenzied seizing upon distinctions and trying to separate them out from unity. It has become an almost pathological behaviour.

THE HERMIT AND THE DRUID

To those who insist on following only a purely spiritual path, I say they are ignoring the fact that the spirit cannot be seen in isolation in this incarnation. We live in a material universe in which we work to integrate spirit and matter holistically.

To say, for instance, that we want to have nothing to do with politics is to ignore the fact that so many of our actions are political and have resonance in the community in which we live - and in other communities too. Even if we shun human contact we live in communion with the universe and we must still make decisions in which we order our priorities in respect of resources necessary to the maintenance of being.

To those who say that they wish only to pursue and develop the cultural is to ignore the fact that the culture of a people consists in their political and spiritual being and how that is made manifest in material things, in movement, song, dance, colour and sovereignty. You can be a hermit. I know a few charming ones. You can be a Druid, equally charming. But you cannot be a hermit and a Druid. If you believe you can you have not grasped the nature of Druidry. The moment you sense the essence of Druidry you cease there and then to be a hermit. This might be a pity because I like hermits, and there are a few Druids I have to admit I find it hard to take.

MAGIC AND TRUTH

Underlying politics, culture, spirit, this world, the Otherworld, art, song, dance, sport, sex, thought, word and deed, along with all the other diverse facets of the universe are the patterns and relationships that constitute what some call the natural order and others the laws of nature.

Understanding and working in concord with those patterns and relationships to achieve some particularly desired end is sometimes known as Magic - quite the opposite to its normal 'supernatural' ascription.

What have Magic and Truth to do with each other? Everything. Magic can be achieved simply, providing it has Truth behind it. I write a letter of Truth against some injustice. I send it to the Editor of a newspaper for publication. He/she publishes it. Others respond against the perceived injustice. They organise, educate, act, coordinate protest. The injustice is removed. Cause and effect - sheer magic - as simple as that. I know. I have written letters and articles over the years. In some cases when published they have had the desired effect. For Truth is also about understanding and working with those patterns and relationships that bind the many facets of the universe holistically. Indeed they might often be one and the same thing. If we were to look for a distinction we would find the following: Magic is the working, Truth is the measure. Magic is when we understand the rightness or fitness of a word, an action, a behaviour, of the way we work and use that understanding to achieve a particularly desired end. Truth is the measure of the rightness or fitness of a word, an action, a behaviour, of the way we live.

WHAT UNIVERSE?

It is all very well talking about the universe and the natural order that underlies it. But what do we mean about "the natural order" of the universe? Are we talking in cosmological terms like Stephen Hawking? Or are we using that term in relation to life itself, plant, animal and human, and its evolution? It is notable that even Stephen Hawking fell back on his high school Darwinism to explain the evolution of life after he and his colleagues so brilliantly explained the Big Bang that created the physical universe. We must ask ourselves - what universe are we talking about? The material lifeless one or the natural one full of life? Stephen Hawking has explained the origin of our universe. He has not explained life, the life force, falling back on Darwin's Origins of the Species to do that. In his own field he is a master, a genius at explaining a lifeless universe. Stephen writes and speaks on the sole basis that his present knowledge of evolution depends entirely on Darwin.

I agree with the late Stephen and his colleagues that there are probably any amount of universes in being, that there are black holes in space that are gateways via connecting 'wormholes' to 'white dwarfs' that lead in turn to baby universes, which can branch anywhere out of our universe and come back in via a black hole and white dwarf to some other part of our universe. For the moment we will stick to our own universe, our own world and our realm of this world. Our universe, our world, our life and our selves are everything.

For the present we can only deal with our own universe until we learn how to travel through black holes, wormholes, white dwarfs, baby universes, even other universes, which our descendants should be doing in a hundred years' time. The black hole in Cygnus X-1, appears to have had more than just a passing interest to those famous watchers of the skies, our ancestral Druids. Naturally. What we are really looking for is a borderline that exists somewhere within the field of human activity, because it is obvious from studying our universe today that some of the things people are doing is causing the breakdown of the natural order, and some of the things people are not doing is holding back the progress of humankind, especially in terms of human-spiritual evolution. There are humans and institutions who are downright obstructionist, who are always holding back human endeavour, leaving no footprints behind them in the sands of time. Their only aim is to preserve the past and present mythos underlying their status quo, thus preserving themselves, their powers, titles, offices - and wealth. Let them be warned: let no man set a boundary to the march of humanity!

THE MYSTIC LAND

To know and understand what is about us and within us we have to shed many ideas about ourselves and the land, the result of centuries of erroneous thought brought into the western world all those centuries ago when the ancient ones could only disappear away, shaking their noble and intelligent heads in sadness at what they knew would inevitably come to pass. The land is not cold and savage. It is not a place of conflict. Savagery is only chosen by savages and man is most capable of that choice. The land is not savage, rather it is the warp of all being. The land is - a pure state that mystics aspire to.

But very few people are, or can afford, to be mystics. And the problem is not solved by gaining the wisdom of the land, dowsing the ley lines and divining the truth. If That were so, we Druids could all go away to our little retreats and lead the most satisfying of lives in pursuit of the greatest intellectual adventure of all, while we let the world and its mother go to hell in a juggernaut. Our knowledge and wisdom is granted to us to take the land into our hands and make the changes. The ability to work real magic is a great and terrible gift fraught with many dangers. But it is one we cannot ignore. Yet even that is not enough. There are many paths to wisdom and the best is the path of working together, guiding, leading and helping to initiate other enlightened souls along the way.

IN THE SERVICE OF DRUIDRY

Druidry is the espousal of a specific set of values divined from an extremely ancient lineage of wisdom. It is these values which form the framework that guides the way in which we use what we have come to understand of the universe, the world and all existences. We may dispute, between ourselves, the finer points of those values, but broadly speaking we must recognise that they are concerned with the maintenance of order.
This is not reactionary for a real understanding of the universe will show that the one constant is change. Nothing is ever still. Nothing remains fixed, not even Einstein's Cosmological Constant. And Einstein, who believed in a non-scriptural God (very Druidic!) famously stated that; "God does not play dice with the universe." Maintaining order consists of understanding the ever-evolving principles of things and that all we do in the universe accords with these principles. We must therefore come to appreciate what is Truth and work to ensure that all our worlds accord with it.

Everything we are as Druids and do as a result is governed by the Truth against the World. Truth is the ultimate standard we aspire to. The World is our work. And that work is Service. Truth and Service are linked. So long as we Druids proclaim the Truth then Druidry is Service. Service, in the past, was ultimately concerned with maintaining a balance - materially, socially, spiritually. It was all about listening to the voice of the land and guiding others. Service must now be restored , showing that the land has a voice waiting to be heard. Do you want to know a secret....listen to those whisperings in your ear.

Explorations

Chapter Twenty One

The Atlantis Archipelago

A site of human civilization was found a decade ago within Ireland's Navan Fort complex which was dated back as far as 7000 B.C., all of nine thousand years ago. Yet people find it hard to accept the Druids as advanced beings who worked the wonders of Newgrange and some other places nearly six thousand years ago. We will continue to unlock their secrets only if we stay attuned and eventually hurtle across time and the astral in a spiritual quantum leap to commune with their spirits. For they were diviners of genius.

Their layouts are occulted because they conceal the secrets of universal physics, the secrets of thought transference and the ultimate secret of existence itself, of the life force manifest in living creatures, of the cosmic plains that we refuse to walk because we choose to see only the world in which the human race so narrowly confines itself. Let the Druid Initiate offer the grail cup of heart and soul to receive the light of the spirit, a cup that will forever overflow as the Initiate progresses as a son of God.

When we are growing into this world we do not suddenly see and understand truth. Truth is eternally there but we have to find it, spending lifetimes seeking the greater mysteries in the depths of ourselves and finding the guidance of the ancient ones in the depths of our being. This is not found suddenly but is achieved by following one path of knowledge and realisation to the next.

The mysteries became known as the path, the light of the way of the Druid. Today people still choose to place themselves on this small old path and find the workings of the life force in truth, peace and love. Sooner or later they come upon the Path of High Druidry, as did the ancient ones, and find themselves in the mystery school of knowledge, and, achieving wisdom at long last, find themselves as adepts in all humility linked by soul consciousness from one to another, with many strange yet wonderful happenings alongside everyday life, enjoying worlds unknown to ordinary man, existences glimpsed by the mystic poet.

To become a Druid Initiate is to stroll along the path of light, crossing over the narrow dogmatic confines of religions, churches and denominations with incredible ease, through golden caverns unknown to worldly man, sailing along emerald seas, crossing rainbow plains, gliding on to crystal towers and lying on the sun-kissed grass amid the timeless groves of great old oaks. Taken only as another leisure interest it is soon an empty illusion. But for the Druid of old this is the path that was gladly embraced as the natural birthright. Girls and boys were chosen to be initiated into the wisdom and the spirit of light was carried from generation to generation. It was easy then, more difficult in today's unnatural world. As we merge our consciousnesses, the 'me' and the 'not me', we are led forward in the understanding of Truth, Love and Service.

THE SHINING ONES

Newgrange is the central powerhouse in the Irish earth energy grid. At some point way back before history began it was closed down and the knowledge lost until now in this new emerging age of Druidic science. The purpose of the cairns was not for sacrifice. As late as the seventh century the doctrinal fallacies of the Church could not allow men the free will we cherish today, so the Druidic mysteries were once again deliberately hidden. It is only now at last in the re-enlightenment of the new age that these mysteries are gradually surfacing as humanity realises that it is not inherently 'sinful' but must make progress, more especially for the sake of our descendants.

We know by now that the Druids used the pendulum, the Ogham and scrying, as well as their mathematics, science and astronomy to great result. They were highly evolved with brilliant minds and great powers, working within a balanced planetary auric energy. In Irish mythology we have the priests of light, the Shining Ones, entering the cairns never to be seen again. Is it possible to separate the accelerated auric body and the life force in a cyclotron-cairn, producing an unknown materialisation that flies off at the speed of light? Are these ancient ones still within our inner space, as our friends, just waiting to be consulted after all these years?

THE LOST ISLANDS OF ATLANTIS

The puzzle of 'The Lost Continent of Atlantis' may be solved at last. It was not a huge continental-type landmass but rather a series of islands stretching from off the west coast of Ireland and right down along the Atlantic seaboard in a vast crescent of an archipelago of now submerged islands off Brittany, France, Spain and Portugal curving out as far as the Azores, the last remnants of Atlantis. The northernmost island of this Atlantis chain is submerged off Valentia Island at latitude 51.42 degrees - the magical angle of the Pyramids! Tir na nOg, The Land of Eternal Youth; Tir faoi Thoinn, the Land beneath the Waves; the magical island of Hy Brasil, visible on a clear day off the west coast of Ireland, after which Brazil is named, are all variously descriptions of that Atlantean island seen by the native Irish thousands of years ago.

And the major east to south=west ley line of telluric force across Ireland flashes out into the Atlantic via Valentia Island and straight across the ocean into the sea area in which the northern tip of the Atlantis Isles would have been. Allowing for coastal erosion over twelve thousand years, sea-going explorers should sail for ninety miles out from Valentia Head to find the submerged remnants of the northernmost island of Atlantis today.

The Great Pyramid is built with Newgrange as an ancient prototype and with Stonehenge as one of its 'ancestors' as well.

It is virtually established now that much of the science of Atlantis is inherent in the pyramids, which as I have just noted, are a later development of the mound of Newgrange in Ireland - the same sacred science and mathematics! It can therefore no longer be fully accepted, if at all, that the Druids and their science, astronomy and mathematics came to Ireland from Europe.

It is now almost certain that the Druids emerged among the pre-Celtic Irish, those known as the Tuatha DeDanaan or probably even earlier among the Formorians. It is now possible to think that Atlantean survivors ,who landed in Ireland after the great flood ,due to the melting of the ice drowning their isles out in the Atlantic, taught the original Druids.

According to the scientists that would have been at least twelve thousand years ago! Graham Hancock 'backdates' the pyramids to the same period in his book, Fingerprints of the Gods, a mighty good read that cannot lightly be denied! Good, it's high time we Irish progressed in explaining the ancient civilisation in our own Boyne valley rather than forever dodging the issue.

As for the Atlanteans, as their fabulous islands off the west coast of Ireland submerged due to the retreating ice, they came in upon the land of Ireland, forced at last to make contact with the native aborigines, with a view possibly to re constructing their new Atlantis in Ireland and across Europe. They travelled through the land of Ireland, teaching the best of the natives over the centuries, These went on to build the cairns, the stone circles and the aligned standing stones, somehow trying to build it all back up again - an Atlantis in Ireland. Over the generations they conveyed their magical science to the best of the native Irish who in turn became the very first Druids in the world.

They built Newgrange. They travelled directly along the powerful ley lines of telluric force from their sunken islands. In time they travelled with Druid hand in hand across the land and across the sea to where the major ley line flashed upon the Sacred Island of Mona, Holy Island, today's Holyhead. Then, turning the circle, they wheeled clockwise and transferred to the major north-south ley line down through Britain.

They built Stonehenge. On they travelled across the Channel, on down through the European landmass, through ancient Greece where they became worshipped as the gods and goddesses of Olympus. Crossing the Mediterranean they entered the Land of Egypt, where they founded and taught the ancient High Priesthood. Such is not only our heritage, it is in our blood, in our genes and in our very Being.
For they lay down with the daughters of our lands and gave birth to the Shining Ones, the priests of light that Irish mythology can only hint at as gods and goddesses.

Beyond the triple spiral, echoing across the aeons from the sacred chamber of Newgrange, the sacred fire at the flash of the solstice light brought forth the most magical children into the world, to lead and guide the land of Ireland, and then the rest of the world. They were the first of the Druids.

Thousands of years later, when the time came, Rome thought it was dealing with a competing religion, an old 'Celtic Church' of the Druids.
Such a 'church' never existed. But the remnants of the pure Atlantean Druidic science did. Rome wrongly regarded that as some sort of idolatry. It still does!

The Atlanteans had no need of a huge vast 'continent' out in the Atlantic or under Antarctica or anywhere else, as Atlantis has always been conceived of up to now. There was no need either for volcanoes, earthquakes, disasters or explosions to originally sink Atlantis. How many islands off Ireland, Scotland, France, Spain and Portugal "beyond the Pillar of Herak-

les" have sunk through the millennia? Now I have the geologists, geographers, geophysicists and even the archaeologists nodding their heads. There are hundreds of records of islands sinking.
The melting of the ice flooded the world and drove the seas to all-time heights, submerging hundreds of islands at the least.

There is nothing at all special about it, nothing except you need no longer scour the Atlantic seabed for remnants of the Lost Continent.

Today all the advanced sophisticated equipment of the U.S.A. could be brought over here and operated off a group of our offshore islands. The NASA space programme, the nuclear, stealth and advanced information and communication systems, the telecommunications and satellite systems, almost every conceivable technological system, could be operated from a group of such offshore islands. The ancients certainly had no need of a vast continent as Atlantis has always been conceived of up to now.

As we know now that 'Lost Continent' never existed, but Atlantis, like a thousand islands off the coast of Ireland, did, and we are all the better for it. We have followed the trail of the serpent and found his head under our feet.

Chapter Twenty Two

Chief Druid of His Time

Darrell Figgis (1882 - 1925)

Born in Dublin and brought up in India, Darrel Figgis was a patriotic Celtic Irish nationalist. Involved with Erskine Childers in the Howth Gun Running of 1914, Figgis was elected a member of the first Dail Eireann in 1918. He was Secretary of Sinn Fein 1917 -1919. A cultural nationalist, Darrell Figgis looked on Horace Plunkett's co-operative movement as a modern equivalent of such ancient institutions operating under the Brehon Laws.

For he was Chief of the Irish Druid Order throughout the fateful years of the fight for Irish freedom until the aftermath of the Irish Civil War. As Chief Druid in a ferociously Catholic Ireland he was inhibited, but he had the good will of several of the Men of '16, Pearse and Plunkett included, and later of George Russell, AE, who he eulogises here, as well as W.B. Yeats and Maud Gonne. Patrick Pearse had been initiated as a Druid at the Cardiff Eisteddfod of 1899 along with Figgis and an Irish delegation.

Although Ireland was in ancient times the Land of the Druids par excellence, up to recently those Irish people who dared to take an interest in Druidry and to call themselves Druids usually had to join in secret the Druid Order of neighbouring Wales. But all of that has changed now.

A prolific poet, naturally after the style of the Fili, Figgis published several books of poems including A Vision of Life (1909) and an Abbey play, Queen Tara (1913).

He wrote Gaelic State Past and Future (1917) and The Historic Case For Irish Independence (1920). He offered volumes of literary criticism too, notably Shakespeare (1911). He also wrote five novels, maintaining a high literary output throughout his short life. Children of the Earth (1918), his study of native Irish character on Achill Island, was admired by Daniel Corkery - in spite of Figgis' stringent review of A Munster Twilight (1916), in the course of which he defined Anglo-Irish literature openly as " the use of the English language in books by Irishmen writing of their own affairs and from their own national point of view". The House of Success (1921) compares an Irish businessman's practical viewpoint with his son's militant nationalism and finds both wanting - based on his own life at the time; he was the scion of wealthy Dublin booksellers. The Return of the Hero (1923), for which James Stephens wrote a foreword, presents the famous colloquy between Oisin and St. Patrick in which Christianity comes off worst.

Darrel Figgis was serving on an Irish Broadcasting Commission, embattled by Catholics demanding strict censorship when, as a result, he was driven to commit suicide in 1925. He is Appleby in Eimar O'Duffy The Wasted Land (1919). He wrote under the pseudonym 'Michael Ireland'. As he writes about his colleague AE here, he is writing prior to the 'Blood Sacrifice of 1916' which was an entirely Druidic eruption upon Dublin at Easter 1916. Figgis writes expertly here too about the Brehon Laws, and we also have AE's famous reply to Rudyard Kipling, two great poets locked briefly in battle on the stage of the world. How fitting for a File!

In the opening paragraph Figgis skillfully analyses the young AE against the unlikely background of a Salvation Army brass band on the pier at Bray one Sunday morning.

The Standish O'Grady mentioned is the famous Irish novelist who knew all his ancient deities as well as any of the others. They were all dwellers in the one grove at one time or another.

    AE
By Darrell Figgis

{Edited and adapted for publication by Michael McGrath)

Standish O'Grady, one fair Sunday in summer, returned home a puzzled and an arrested man. He brought with him the news that he had heard, on the sea-front at Bray, the bearded figure of a young man in a tweed suit addressing the human flood before him, evangelising (if one may use that word) the ancient pagan gods of Ireland. It was a lone spectacle.

The sight of other young men, lit by a later faith and loud with tunes that made up in clamour what they lacked in music, or others more brightly apparelled, with big drums and brass instruments twisted into the likeness of the serpents they fought would have been appropriate enough to the scene. They would not have attested the least incurious. Besides that, they would have been gregarious: they would have fortified themselves with bigness as they fortified themselves with loudness. This other was quite another thing. Spectacularly it was lonely.
Lifted into the imagination it was lonelier yet; and something tragic withal. Its inappropriateness was its occasion, but that very fact gave it a gesture strange and appealing, gave it a voice that was like a slender rune of music that had wandered out of its place.

What did these people, with one half of their devotions over for the day, or with the height of their weekly holiday come, want to know of Earth, the mother of us all, the Dana of ancient reverence, on whose bosom they trod unheedingly, having first hidden it beneath asphalt, like fleas on some elephant's back, thinking nothing of the great life, the deep knowledge, the throb of power beneath them; or of the great Shining Ones that are housed within her or that throng the heavenly places in hierarchy on hierarchy of brightness and beauty and power, dimly perceived and dimly reverenced under many an ancient name in days when reverence had not been withered by tawdry pleasure, a huckster's vulgar gain, or the desperate oath from slumdom? Were they not the heirs of civilization? Had they not religions cut and suited to their order - or the order of their masters? Who then was this strange, wild man, whom they would not hear, and whom some few of them may have recognised as a clerk at Pim's and a mere shop assistant accordingly? What to them was the shining Lugh? This man at least was no Lugh, they would have rashly agreed. What of Balor? Balor, if they had heard of him, was, like Lugh, a myth;

- and they did not know themselves to be held in his one-eyed spell. As for Manannan, whose lips so carelessly caressed the shore, could they not push their skiffs out upon his waters, and make the rowlocks, if need were, stain in contempt of such an one? Besides, the man, though young, was not shaven. Plainly a peculiar case. Standish O'Grady's thoughts are not recorded. We do not know if he felt like Oisin, that he would rather be with Finn and Caoilte in hell than with Patrick's God who took so queer a delight in burning. Very likely he did.

Very likely he felt his place was rather beside this lonely figure than with the driftage of which he formed a part. It needs no imagination, however, to conceive that he felt less as if he had seen a strange sight than as if he had looked upon a portent. For the voice of ancient Ireland was speaking through this man; and speaking in an Anglicized watering-place.

In truth, it was a portent; and if Standish O'Grady had been the wise man we know him to be, he would have prayed, even without committing himself to the religious fire that burned in the young man's soul, that the portent might be of happy omen. For the social doctrine which it lit, and of which it formed an inevitable part, gave it a shrewdness of application. This was no fantastic faith that was being declared. Nor was this man an esoteric mystic.

Life seen through the eyes of a man concerned for ideals, that is to say, through the eyes of a man to whom religion is quite other than a matter of formal belief, resolves itself into something very sane and very clean. It's essential, and because essential always possible, dignity and splendour are not to be waived by reference to modern complexities.

Idealists are often quick logicians: this idealist particularly was so; and it would not avail to commit the first of logical fallacies by begging the very issue that was at debate. To create a degrading complexity, and then to argue the complexity in defence of the degradation, was hardly a procedure that would at any time, then or now, have confused for the preacher of the Bray promenade the battle in which he was engaged.

Man the child of Dana, and man crushed by a vast and nightmare engine, were not for him two persons, but one and the same person. Earth did not differentiate, though it was pitifully, tragically true that where some of her children bowed themselves before her others failed from her. Therefore would he not differentiate.

And so a social doctrine emerged in these Bray disclosures that was shrewd in its simplicity, and worldly-wise because earthly-wise in its arrangement of a life that had fallen from greatness.

It was not from books that this came: certainly not from the writings of men who in those years prostrated themselves before the accomplished fact of degradation and saw in it the fine flower of civilization. As AE confesses, between the ages of eighteen and thirty he hardly so much as read a newspaper; though that the affairs of his country did not pass unheeded many of his writings at that time show clearly. His life was one of mystical experiment and experience: of study over the writings of ancient seers and initiates into the mysteries of the heavens and the earth, and over a wisdom once dearly cherished but now almost relinquished for the passions of the body and the irritations of the intellect; of a very rare circle of friendship that came finally, before its members were scattered through the world, almost a community of mind; and of a larger circle that acknowledged his leadership - we may hope - not too obsequiously - that turned to him for counsel, and accepted, it would appear, almost a spiritual dictatorship.

Four men who lived so rich, again because so experiential, a life together that they grew to something like a community of personality, where each was the fuller because of the others, each giving his dividual and essential quality, where yet none could have a strict privy life because the community attained was so complete that Their interchanges could dispense with words -this plainly is a matter that challenges to be divulged.

And when it is remembered that the experiences and experiments that formed the groundwork of this community were mystical wisdom, discovered anew or housed in ancient writings, clearly the matter must be left to rest very tenderly as it was, though others who had to fight a somewhat lonely hand might covet the tale that would be told.

The only light we are suffered, other than that the mind engenders by brooding on the relation, is given in an incident related in a magazine to which they all, in the circle of which they formed a part, content it was not told "because it is extraordinary,"but "because it was a revelation of the secret of power, a secret with which the wise in good and the wise in evil alike have knowledge of, and it is told , as we divine, of one of that community who had come to a crisis in his spiritual life in which "two paths were open before him." "On one side lay the dazzling mystery of passion; on the other 'the small old path' held out its secret and spiritual allurements. I had hope," he says, that his friend "would choose the latter, and as I was keenly interested in his decision , I invested the struggle going on in his mind as something of universal significance."

"He came in late one evening. I saw at once by the dim light that there was something strange in his manner. I spoke to him in enquiry; he answered me in a harsh dry voice quite foreign to his usual manner: 'Oh I am not going to trouble myself any more, I will let things take their course' .....I soon saw what had happened; his mind, in which forces so evenly balanced had fought so strenuously, had become utterly wearied out and could work no longer. A flash of old intuition illuminated it at last - it was not wise to strive with such bitterness over life -therefore he said to me in memory of this intuition, 'I am going to let things take their course'. A larger tribunal would decide. I sent him up to his room and tried to quiet his fever with magnetization with some success.

He fell asleep, and as I was rather weary myself! retired soon after."

To sleep came vision. In a "space opened on every side with pale, clear light," "a slight wavering figure caught my eye, a figure that swayed to and fro; I was struck with its utter feebleness, yet I understood it was its own will or some quality of its nature which determined that palpitating movement towards the poles between which it swung." Above this figure "two figures awful in their power, opposed each other; the frail being wavering between them could by putting out its arms have touched them both. It alone wavered, for they were silent, resolute, and knit in the conflict of will:; they stirred not a hand nor a foot; there was only a still quivering now and then as of intense effort, but they made no other movement. Their heads were bent forward slightly, their arms folded, their bodies straight, rigid, and inclined slightly backwards from each other like two spokes of a gigantic wheel." These two "were the culminations of the human towering images of the good and evil man may aspire to. I looked at the face of the evil adept. His bright red-brown eyes burned with a strange radiance of power; I felt an answering emotion of pride, of personal intoxication, of psychic richness, rise up within me, gazing on him. His face was archetypal: the abstract pattern, which eluded me in the features of many people I knew, was here declared, exultant, defiant, giantesque; it seemed to leap like fire, to be free. In this face I was close to the legendary past, to the hopeless worlds where men were martyred by stony kings, where prayer was hopeless, where pity was none. I traced a resemblance to many of the great destroyers in history whose features have been preserved, Napoleon, Rameses, and a hundred others, named and nameless, the long line of those who were crowned and sceptred in cruelty. His strength was in human weakness - I saw this, for space and the hearts of men were bare before me. Out of space there flowed to him a stream half invisible of red: it nourished that rich, radiant energy of passion:

it flowed from men as they walked and brooded in loneliness, or as they tossed in sleep."

From this figure he turned to the other. An aura of pale, soft blue was around this figure, though which gleamed an underlight as if of universal gold . . ...I caught a glimpse of a face godlike in its calm, terrible in the beauty of a life we know only in dreams, with strength which is the end of the hero's toil, which belongs to the many times martyred soul . . ... I understood how easy it would have been for this one to have ended the conflict, to have gained a material victory by its power, but this would not have touched on or furthered its spiritual ends. Only its real being had force to attract that real being which was shrouded in the wavering figure. This truth the adept of darkness knew also, and therefore he intensified within the sense of pride and passionate personality. Therefore they stirred not a hand nor a foot while under the stimulus of their presence culminated the good and evil in the life which had appealed to a higher tribunal to decide. Then this figure wavering between the two moved forward and touched with its hand the Son of Light. All at once the scene and actors vanished, and the eye that saw them was closed. ; I was alone with darkness and a hurricane of thoughts."

Dreams are sometimes the body's torment: more happy they are the spirit's liberation; and here in dream one friend saw the issue that befell another in the deep world whence Life takes its rise, for the after-days revealed the fact that the conflict had been so decided. It tells little, yet a little , of what lay behind in the friendship it revealed: and it was only told, as it is told at some length here, because of the help it might give to others in like issue, for "although the gods and cosmic powers may war over us for ever, it is we alone declare them victors or vanquished; but in it we may also see not a little of the conflicts of the inner life of those days, in the nest of that friendship and in the spiritual history of the man who was to emerge to more public hours.

The mind distantly perceives that such a community, once it was attained, would have to be broken before stagnation, or uniformity which is the same thing, should succeed; and when that happened one of that community was left in Ireland because his life belonged to Ireland, where one feels that the others did not. Born in Lurgan, in the County Armagh, on

10th April, 1867, he came to the City of Dublin when he was about seven or eight years of age. He was put to school in Rathmines. At the age of sixteen AE passed to the School of Art.

It was here that he met W.B. Yeats, who was then prolific of verse, not having arrived at the caution of later years, and who, as a page of reminiscence recalls, "had a tendency to chant his verses to all in heaven and earth." They became friends. Both were Art students; and it was AE's desire then to follow that gleam. The Master of Life had another decision; and the following year found him in Pim's, a drapery house of the city.

THE BREHON LAWS

The Feineacas or Brehon Laws, which image for us the old Irish State, have never received the attention they deserve, and there is a political reason for that. They have been edited with misconceiving and belittling introductions from an English point of view, and with translations altered from those made by the far finer Irish scholars O'Donovan and O'Curry. The Napoleonic Code, The Roman Code, even that' far removed Hammurabi Code, have not failed of adequate exposition, whereas the Feineacas have not yet taken their place in international comparison, though they challenge comparison with any in a noble conception of Life.

(Dr. Dwyer argues, as others do, that the Brehon Laws have never been declared illegal in Ireland, neither in the Republic nor in Northern Ireland. Certainly I have never read about or heard of any such declaration -author). Yet how did they come to be? Those other laws were, as all other laws have been, abstractly conceived in legislative assembly or princely edict, and abstractly codified. Yet in none of them is there an arresting idea of Life. They are just workaday administrative instruments, all that a lawyer would desire, though, being abstractly conceived, there was both time and opportunity to introduce into them some higher ideal. The Feineacas, on the other hand, are just a medley of ad hoe adjudications, the rough gathering together of judgements, given by Brehons in their functions as civil arbitrators, hard to disentangle in their lack of systematic form. Yet, what is the result? Arising as they do from the clash of life in its least savoury aspects, emerging as they do from disputes and wrangles and their settlements, they yet display a conception of Life that arrests the mind with its dignity, humanity and decency.

It was left to this latter time (Here Figgis means his own period immediately before the 1916 Dublin Rebellion -author) to evolve, outside of Parliament, and despite the bitter opposition of Irishmen whose minds are subdued to English thinking, a distinctive Irish polity, the Feineacas beginning to be reborn in modern conditions, to construct an Irish State out of the practical experience of life, and to oppose English civilization, that is already self-condemned, with a distinctive Irish conception of civilization that has some hope for the future. And it is to AE that the praise for this is due more than to any other. For what are his Rural Communities? They are neither more nor less than a reconstitution of the Tuatha , the economic, social and political units of the old 'tribal' organization of ireland.

"We have not had a social order since the time of the clans", he says in Co-operation and Nationality; and he is right. In The Rural Community he says: "We had true rural communities in ancient Ireland, though the organization was military rather than economic.; but there he is wrong.

The Tuath was hardly even military in a secondary sense, and certainly it was not so primarily. From early times a certain form of Tuath could claim the complete subordination of military duties to their economic life: they could not be called away at Spring or at Harvest, and, if at other times, a provincial hosting should last for more than six weeks, at the end of that six weeks they had liberty to return home. Therefore the Fianna was raised as a national militia from the older Firbolgs and Cruithni, or Picts, and were part of the army with which the great Niall of the Nine Hostages harassed and defeated the Roman power throughout Britain and into Gaul. Cuchulainn, the 'little dark man' and Lord of the Marches to Conchubhair, was such a man. When later they were suppressed for political reasons it was the very economic preoccupation of the Tuatha that made them the prey of the Normans who were professional marauders devoid of any economic life. And as the economic life of the Tuatha still restricted their military power, foreign soldiers (gall oglaigh, Englished into Gallowglasses, means foreign soldier) were imported and settled on the land by the consent of the Tuatha to relieve them of the continual fighting to which they were compelled by the presence of this professional marauder. These galloglaigh came from the Hebrides, and were thus descended from the Irish conquest of the Isles mixing with earlier and later Norse.

In the Tuath the lowest form of un-freeman was the Fuidhir. He was lower than the jack-boys and hirelings of the Tuath, being generally a prisoner taken in war or an outlaw from some other Tuath. Yet the Feineacas allowed him to join in some company of not less than five, to hold land together. Wouldn't such a scheme afford unemployed people a break today, a gleam of light at the end of the tunnel, if our own society were worthy enough to afford a way out to our latter-day slaves. It is true that these Fuidhir were the first enthusiastic converts who flocked to Patrick.

Druid Soul and Psyche

We are more than we appear to be. The world is more than it appears to be. Mankind, generally speaking, is very limited in its awareness of what is going on. Parapsychology is an attempt to work at the edges of it, to find out more about what we are. I believe that some bio-energy field - what is referred to as the aura that creates psychic phenomena - surrounds every human being. This field can affect healing and is responsible for phenomena such as telepathy, telekinesis and precognition. This field is the soul whose core is the psyche. It is connected to the body during the body's brief lifetime, disconnects itself at death and is eternal. Our body is just the vehicle it uses during this particular phase of its existence. And it comes back and attaches itself to another vehicle. This, as you know, is called reincarnation.

There is an overall meaning to everybody's existence, which is this constant cycle of living, dying, coming back. We are headed somewhere - back to where we came from initially, when we were perfect in a real sense.

I am sure you and your loved ones read each other's minds most of the time. This is a living psychic experience. When people are married a long time, when they live together as families for a long time, this energy field I speak of, which they all have, becomes so strongly intertwined that, when one of them dies, it's like having a huge living chunk taken out of the survivors. It is not just grief that survivors are feeling. I think this is why people who are very close sometimes die within days of each other.

Strabo, for instance, states that the Druids "have pronounced that men's souls and the universe are indestructible." Pomponius Mela is more specific about the teaching of the Druids:

One of their dogmas has come to common knowledge, namely, that souls are eternal and that there is another life in the infernal regions, and this has been permitted manifestly because it makes the multitude readier for war. And it is for this reason too that they burn or bury, with their dead, things appropriate to them in life; and that in times past they even used to.defer the completion of business and the payment of debts until their arrival in another world. Indeed, there were some of them who flung themselves willingly on the funeral pyres of their relatives in order to share the new life with them.

From this it would seem that the afterlife is not regarded as a sad or dull place in Druidic philosophy, but rather a new, vital and valuable sphere of existence. Lucan, who pessimistically believes in the cold Roman afterlife ruled by the god Pluto, defiantly throws out his challenge to the Druids: And you, O Druids, now that the clash of battle is stilled, once more have you returned to your barbarous ceremonies and to the savage uses of your holy rites. To you alone it is given to know the truth about the gods and deities of the sky, else you alone are ignorant of this truth. The innermost groves of far-off forests are your abodes. And it is you who say that the shades of the dead seek not the silent land of Erebus and the pale halls of Pluto; rather, you tell us that the same spirit has a body again elsewhere, and that death, if what you sing is true, is but the midpoint of long life.

In this hostile challenge Lucan, who like most Romans, has no answers of his own, openly sneers at the Druids for claiming that the afterlife is much more cheerful than that described in Greek philosophy. Significantly, he also indicates here that the Druids believe that the body after death is not the old one - as Catholic belief teaches it will be at 'The last Judgment'. In Druidic belief there is no Last Judgment. The attitude of the druids is that the afterlife is a very real one, very like life in this world. Classical intellectuals were amazed by this, especially by Druids looking forward to carrying out commercial dealings in the next life. Valerius Maximus, like Lucan and Mela, writing in the first century AD writes:

It is said that they lend to each other sums that are repayable in the next world, so firmly are they convinced that the souls of men are immortal.

Intermingling of the living and the dead, moving between three worlds, this world, the Otherworld and the next world, these were the concerns of Druidic belief in Ireland as well as wherever Druids walked. And it is now emerging that the Druids were divine teachers indeed. In a recent book Bloodline of the Holy Grail the author Laurence Gardner describes the Druids as the teachers of the children of Jesus: In this recent book that claims to reveal the hidden lineage of Jesus, Gardner says:

We have already seen that Jesus and Mary Magdalene's younger son, Josephes, attended a Druidic college. Educational institutions of the kind were internationally renowned; there were no fewer than sixty such colleges and universities in Europe, boasting a total of more than 60,000 students. The druid priests were not a part of the Celtic Church, but were an established, cohesive element in the structure of Gaelic society in Gaul, Britain and Ireland. They were described by the writer Strabo in the F 1 century BC as 'students of nature and moral philosophy '. He (Strabo) continued:

They are believed to be the most just of men, and therefore are entrusted with judgements in decisions that affect both individuals and the public at large. In former times they arbitrated in war, able to bring to a standstill opponents on the point of drawing up in line of battle; murder cases have very frequently been entrusted to their adjudication.

The Sicilian, Diodorus, another writer of the time, described the Druids as "great philosophers and theologians, who are treated with special honour". The Druids were in addition said to be exceptional statesmen and divine seers. One ancient text states:

The early Christians believed in reincarnation until the Church Council of Constantinople decided against it in 554 AD. But the Celtic Church was free to believe in reincarnation until the Council of Whitby in 664 AD and in fact believed in it long afterwards - tight into the present day! Poets, including Shelley and Vaughan, have grieved over the loss of innocence with which they were cloth when they first came into the world. This idea of a pre-natal existence has its origin in Platonic, Pythagorean and indeed in our own ancient Druidic philosophies.

Here is the Druidic belief in the reincarnation of the immortal soul. And, naturally, it is in accord with the Christian belief that immediately succeeded. No poet, not even AE at his best, has been able to suggest more than a distant retreating echo of the incomparable experience that awaits you. Commencement of the fresh new life, when the soul having been lifted up on high and seen things not lawful to tell, only then may the true nature of all life be seen. Pierced by a wealth of wisdom and bliss and clarity, only then may the world be seen for what it is.

Hitherto the eyes of your soul were closed and blind and frightened, ignorantly dumb, you have been whirled on the ever-circling wheel of life and pain.

With the attainment of angelic splendour, your centre of consciousness having forever been exalted beyond your ego, a flood of ecstasy causes the realisation that it is only the angel who has always been your psyche never before known. No longer does the angel enshrine you like the distant walls of the starry abyss, but he burns ardently within your core, pouring through the channels of your senses an unending stream of bright glory and delight. The gates of your mind are unlocked and swing back upon the hinges, and the celestial realm into which the angel ushers your soul is abundantly and ecstatically disclosed.

Ammianus Marcellinus recorded: " The Druids who, united in a society, occupied themselves with profound and sublime questions, raised themselves above human affairs and sustained the immortality of the soul. The soul descended into the womb of nature to be reborn in another body." Lord Brougham held that "the Ancients all believed in the soul's pre-existence." Theosophists hold that Druids recognised the Karmic Land.

Pythagoras was told by the Irish Druid Abaris (from the Irish Abhras - Doubt; therefore Abaris -Doubter - Philosopher), when they met at present-day Marseille, that he believed in " One great divinity alone who is everywhere since He is in all".

John Scotus Eriugena, the Irish philosopher of the 9th century who was an important gatherer of Druidic knowledge, spoke of God as the essence of all things, of the Divine Dark and the Supreme Nothing, of creation being an eternal unfolding of the Divine Nature, of all things resolved or self-drawn to God.

In describing the beliefs fostered by the Druids, Diodorus Siculus describes how "some people at Celtic burials cast upon the pyre letters written to their dead relative, in the belief that the dead will be able to read them." These would have been, because of the Druidic prohibition on the writing of their own affairs, private family letters to loved ones. Diodorus affirms the Druidic belief in reincarnation:

At dinner the Celts are wont to be moved by chance remarks towards disputes, and, after a challenge, to fight in single combat, regarding their lives as naught. For the belief of Pythagoras is strong among them, that the souls of men are immortal, and that after a definite number of years they live a second life when the soul passes into another body.

RESOURCES

The ancient Druids did not use the Tarot, rather the Ogham. Nor did Merlin. This is no reason why you should not. In fact my own favourite is the Crowley Thoth Tarot. The only professional Tarot book to use is The Book of/ Thoth by Crowley himself. The only 'independent' Tarot book worth your while is Tarot, Mirror of the Soul by Gerd Ziegler, on the Thoth Tarot. Tarot depends on your taste.

The Celtic Tree Oracle works with the sacred trees of the Druids and the Ogham. Liz
& Collin Murray, Rider 1989. Contact Liz Murray, 76 Antrobus Road, Chiswick, London W 4 5NQ. She is also Liaison Officer of the Council of British Druid Orders.

Publications

Network (Ireland) Ruth Marshall, Ballydonahane, Bodyke, Clare, Ireland. Druid/ore Rollo Maughfling, Dove Cottage, Barton-St-David, Somerset, England Awen The Loyal Arthurian Warband, BCM GAIA London WCiN 3XX
The Cauldron Caemorgan Cottage, Cardigan, Dyfed, Wales.

THE ORDER OF DRUIDS IN IRELAND

The Order of Druids in Ireland does not subscribe to 'Wicca' nor does it see itself as 'pagan', rather as representative of the intellectual heritage of Ireland and its Druids in the world today. It is a teaching Order and celebrates the festivals. The Order has the three traditional grades of Bard (File), Ovate (Faith) and Druid (Drui na hEireann). Contact : PhotographerOfKilkenny@gmail.com,, mobile 0877560725

Major Druid Orders

To find the Druid Order, Circle or Grove nearest to you and most suitable to your requirements contact Liz Murray, Liaison Officer, CBDO, 76 Antrobus Road, Chiswick, London W4 5NQ who will assist you. CBDO, The Council of British Druid Orders issues publications and co-ordinates the festivals at Glastonbury, Stonehenge, Avebury, Woodhenge, Primrose Hill and Parliament Hill in London, and throughout England and parts of Wales. Serving Druidry on a daily basis, the Council involves itself in forward planning, projects, and negotiating with English Heritage.

CBDO organises the massive Midsummer Day Festival of Stonehenge, which now attracts 15,000 celebrants every year. The Council has Irish, Welsh, Breton, French, Dutch and North American Associates. The most prestigious Druidic Authority in the world and the most influential too. (Liz Murray is the widow of one of the greatest English Druids of the twentieth century, the late Colin Murray, Druid Coll Hazel Wand. He ran The Golden Section Order, a Druidic version of The Golden Dawn).

The Order of Bards, Ovates and Druids, This Order is now dedicated to uniting Druids and Wiccans in common pagan worship, admitting Wiccans to its Ovate grade. We hear of a great coincidence - or is it? - that their new Chosen Chief lives only a few miles in Kilkenny, Ireland, from the Chief of the Order of Druids in Ireland and our Marble City Grove!

The Glastonbury Order of Druids, Dove House, Barton-St-David, Somerset TA I 1 6DF England. Chosen Chief is the Archdruid of Stonehenge and Britain Rollo Maughfling. Issues Druidlore magazine, the best colourful arty Druid magazine in the world with the best photographs by Rollo's lady wife, the late Archdruidess Donna Brooke (costs £3, back numbers available phone 01458-850924). Rollo directly organises the Stonehenge Midsummer Day Festival. He is the most outspoken Archdruid. His Order is noted for its highly talented Arch Druidesses, the writer Jackie Patterson (The Memory of Trees) and the fabulous Druidic artist Una Woodruff. By far the most active English Druid Order out in the countryside, Rollo is a descendant of the great Irish patriot Charles Stewart Parnell and is Titular Irish Archdruid of Avondale and Wicklow. For the active outdoor type this is the Order to join. It is Rollo Maughfling who finally convinced English Heritage to open Stonehenge on Midsummer Day, not only to select Druid Orders, such as his own but to everybody in the British Isles to worship their own deities and practice their own religion at Stonehenge on the most sacred of days. Indeed such is the great work done by the Glastonbury Order of Druids that, were I living in England, I would have no hesitation in joining this, the very best of British Druid Orders. This Archdruid of Stonehenge and Britain, Rollo Maughfling, is of the line of Merlin - some swear after meeting him that he is in fact Merlin!

Rollo was one of the founders of the Council of British Druid Orders back in 1991 and remains to this day as a pillar of the Council on which he sits as Stonehenge Officer. He has written so many published articles and essays on Stonehenge and Druidry, that were they gathered together into a volume it would be wonderful, The Loyal Arthurian Warband, The L.A.W. A

full Druid Order based on King Arthur, Merlin and the Knights of the Round Table. The Founder/Leader changed his name by deed poll to King Arthur Uther Pendragon back in 1991 and since then has emerged as the champion of civil liberties in England. At the last count he had won 28 court cases under the ancient common law of England, defeating the government's Criminal Justice Act in the High Court. Fighting to defend the trees and reclaim the streets (especially Downing Street!) King Arthur leads the most active of all British Orders by a mile! He has replaced the late Screaming Lord Sutch at the polls. His life story is told in his book The Trials of Arthur. His knights are organised into three ranks, numbering 3000. Martial arts and sword fighting are practised. If you love Merry England this is the life for you. Contact 10 Sine Close, Farnborough, Hampshire GU 14 8HG Tel. 01252-544746. You are guaranteed to see active service. Heroic knights are decorated and promoted! While filming in England, writer Ken Kesey (One Flew over the Cuckoo 's Nest) and friends were knighted by King Arthur as they joined his merry Druid band. This is the fastest growing Druid Order in the world at the time of writing. No wonder!
(Member of CBDO).
(Arthur's Story The Trials of Arthur is in the bookshops a compelling read).

The Secular Order of Druids. This Order was born when its Chief, Tim Sebastian, a Druid harpist, started to marry people on stage to the reverb of rock bands during the open air festivals. Tim still marries couples according to the ancient Druidic Rite, but these days he is more likely to be seen worshipping the Goddess with the music of his harp. For the Secular Order of Druids is now the most Goddess-oriented of all the English Orders. A quiet and serious Druid, Tim is a past Chairman of the Council of British Druid Orders. This is the Order to join for the contemplative Druid who is devoted to the Goddess. There are no intellectual pretensions, no London literary Druids, no martial artists, no fame - just the peace of the Grove. I know Druids who would gladly settle for that -the wise ones! Ah, I can feel the peace coming on.

The Insular Order of Druids. This is the Free Welsh Order of Druids resident in England under its Chosen Chief in exile . These are the descendants of the magnificent ancient Welsh Druids, who are not merely Bards like the large official body back home in Wales.

ULSTER DRUIDS.

On our return to Tara in 1993 we were pleased to celebrate the summer solstice on Tara with Ian Carter Long and the Belfast Grove of Druids.

The Berengarian Order of Druids. Women rule O.K! These are the Cat People, these are the fabulous women of Berengaria in the London of the future. Men could join but they wouldn't last an hour among these lovely Druidesses. No you may not have their address, you will have to apply to the Liaison Officer of CBDO for that - and convince her of your bona fides before you go any further. Having said all this, the Berengarians are very serious Druids indeed, and omnipotent too. They are not Wiccans, far too wise for that. Heady stuff (Member of CBDO).

The Stargrove Order of Druids. Led by that formidable Archdruidess, Jackie Huxter Freer and her husband, this Druid Order claims to have the best starlore of all, and most Druids agree. I have seen their course of instruction and it seems to me to be the best in England. This is the Order for the potential astrologer to join, or if you simply want to know on a continual lifelong basis what the stars hold for you. Better still it is a teaching Order which means that it will have you up and running as a Druid or Druidess as fast as you can learn. Stargrove is based in London for oral teaching in the traditional Druid way and to observe the festivals of the Eightfold Druidic Year. Tel 0181 - 840 - 4656 or write to Jackie Huxter Freer, BM Stargrove, London WCiN 3XX. Bring your telescope, binoculars at least - you'll need them!

The Druids of Silures, This is an authentic Grove of Welsh Druids, the Free Druids of Wales. Their Chosen Chief Neil Powell is a most powerful Druid of Wales, certainly more authoritative than the present Archdruid of Wales, who after all is only the Chief Bard of Wales (the official Welsh Order has no Druid grade). But Druid Powell is a fully-fledged Master Druid with aeons of experience behind him. He usually serves as Chief Scribe of the Council of British Druid Orders, so he may be contacted via CBDO, or at home at 2 Woodland Street, Spring Vale, Cwmbran, Gwent NP 44 3AH Wales. Tel 01633 - 873661. (Member of CBDO)

The British Druid Order.

Contact Philip Shallcrass, C11osen Chief, The British Druid Order, 47 Battle Road, St. Leonards-on-Sea, East Sussex, England TN 37 7YP.
The Ancient Druid Order (D.O.). This is the original English Order with ancient lineage direct from the 1717 AD Druid revival in the Appletree Tavern at Covent Garden. Today it is fronted by one of the most formidable Druids in England, David Loxley and Druidess Emma Restall-Orr the writer. It has a highly active membership. Contact the Chosen Chief, David Loxley, 61 Auckland Road, London SE 19 2RH. Yes, these are your authentic Eastenders with a big membership in London Town. Masters of ritual and ceremonial, The Ancient Order of Druids (A.O.D.). Henry Hurle, carpenter, of Garlich Hill, London founded this Order in 1786. Like others it is a benevolent Masonic society for the working and middle classes. Declaredly Christian, it keeps the Bible on its altars. Winston Churchill was initiated as a Druid of this Order in 1908. With the removal of the Papal prohibition on Catholics joining Masonic societies, Catholics may now in conscience join this Order, and all the others like it. The A.O.D. has thousands of members in England. This is the Order for those who want to become Druids while retaining their Christianity. Contact the National Secretary, Rodger Hudson, A.O.D., 174 Tomkinson Road, Nuneaton (near Birmingham), Warwickshire, England. (Member of CBDO).

The United Ancient Order of Druids (U.A.O.D.) Separated from A.O.D. in 1833 and is the largest, richest and most successful Order in the world with 133,000 members and as many affiliates. This Order is primarily a benevolent society and as such it runs businesses including a successful motor insurance company. However, the UAOD. is one the very best Orders for the Druid who travels and wants to socialise with kindred spirits worldwide.

It is organised throughout Britain, Europe, U.S.A., Australia and New Zealand, as well as in more exotic locations. (It is to organise in Ireland this year). It is also a Christian Order with the Bible on its altars and, as the Papal prohibition on Freemasonry no longer applies, membership of the UAOD has begun to rise again in recent years. The Order Statement says that it stands for Unity, Peace and Concorde and its teachings are contained in an interesting book called, The Seven Lessons of Merlin. In America and Australasia, it runs lovely enjoyable social occasions for its family members when everybody robes as druids for the festivals, throws parties and there are barbecues on the lawns.

The children love it as the times of King Arthur, Merlin and the Knights of the Round Table are re-enacted. There are welcome signs that the more progressive elements want to get involved in real Druidry. Those adventurous elements, desirous of partaking in the spirit of genuine Druidry are more than welcome to contact us, and all such contact shall be private and confidential. In fact there has already been such contact at a high level from the UAOD in Europe. Contact the Secretariat-General of the UAOD, 8 Perry Road, Bristol BS I 5BQ, Bristol, England. The address of the Imperial Grand Lodge is 63 Northumberland Avenue, Cliftonville, Margate, KentCT9 3LY.

Then there is the International Grand Lodge of Druids (ILGD), which is the controlling authority of the AOD and the UAOD. In fact they are all interconnected around the globe, which is a positive boon for the Druid traveller. The UAOD admits women members. It has a valuable family membership programme. It's enjoyable.

The London Druid Group/ Universal Druid Order This is also a Masonic society with the important difference that it admits women members - a middle-class English lady administers it. The group is more Druidic than most and celebrates the festivals of the eightfold year in Conway Hall in the centre of London. Everybody is most welcome to these celebrations and this is the ideal group for busy people working and living in central London to join. Again, with the lifting of the Papal prohibition, Catholics may now in all good conscience join this Order. The London Druid Group also holds some of the better lectures, talks and debates on matters Druidic and esoteric. When I phoned this group to make enquiry, the lady who replied to me was most courteous and helpful. So, full marks to the London Druid Group for their excellent good manners! Directly descended from the famous Druidic revival meeting in the Appletree Tavern in Covent Garden in 1717 as assembled by the famous John Toland, the London Druid Group is led today by John Paternoster, 29 Long Meadow, Bishops Stortford, Hertfordshire, CM 23 4HH, England. (Member of CBDO).

While "in London" I would like to mention what I consider to be a most exciting recent development. Druid Orders, Circles, Groves and 'independent' Druids in the capital now get together most weekends at such sites as Parliament Hill and Primrose Hill, fully robed for ritual, ceremonial and really enjoyable social gatherings afterwards. Everyone is absolutely welcome to these impromptu affairs. Contact Liz Murray, CBDO (address above) for information. These gatherings have now become the most enjoyable social aspect of Druidry anywhere in the world with the most renowned guest speakers, celebrants, music and Bards.,.-

Briefly, I now give contacts with the smaller groups. In fact these may be of more help in teaching and training Druids than the larger Orders as they will have much more time on their hands for individuals. In fact you may be lucky in one of these smaller groups to be offered oral training as a Bard, Ovate or Druid in the traditional one-to-one manner as in ancient times. I was lucky to be trained and initiated in this way. It definitely beats any correspondence course hands do\.\n!

Rollo Maughfling will put you in touch with the Cotswold Order of Druids.

Dr. Ronald Hutton, Professor of History at the University of Bristol, will also have contacts among the smaller Druid Orders and Groves. He is the distinguished author of The Triumph of the Moon as well as six other beautifully written works.

The Druid Clan of Dana, Grove of the Four Elements, although based in London. It has its international headquarters of the High Priestess of the Fellowship of Isis, Huntingdon Castle, Clonegal,, Ireland. Although the Druid Clan of Dana. is small, its mother the Fellowship of Isis has a large membership worldwide. Contact the FOI directly or Steve Wilson (of the famous occult Atlantis Bookshop in central London), PO Box 196, London WC I A, 2DY. Steve is also Media Officer of the Council of British Druid Orders, CBDO. He is an accomplished Bard.

Kabbalistic English Druids. This group practises a potent mixture of Druidry and the Kabbalah. Contact Jake Strathom Kent, Park House, Batcombe, Ceme Abbas, Dorchester, Dorset DT2 7BG, England.

The Iolo Morganwg Fellowship. Welsh Druidry at its best! Contact Douglas Lyne, 1 Tite Street, Chelsea, London SW3 4JU (Member of CBDO).

Aos Dana. Scottish Druidry to the Bard grade. Fiona Davidson, Invergowrie House, Ninewells, Dundee DD2 1UA, Scotland.(Honoured Associate of CBDO)
The Taliesin Foundation. Christopher Davies, Gooioord 273, 1103 CR Amsterdam, Netherlands. Also Utrecht. Modem Druidry is beginning to flourish in Holland.

Ecole Druidique des Gaules, The Druidic College of Gaul. Contact Bernard Jacquelin, Villa Montmorency, 75016 Paris, France. Best of the French Druids.

Oaled Drouized Kornog - The Triple Order of Brittany. Contact Bernard Duval, 37 La Vallee, 35720 Saint-Pierre-de-Plesguen, Brittany, and Alain Rouquette, 40 rue de l'Abbesse, 29630 Plougasnou, Brittany.

Gorsedd Kernow. This is the Order of the Druid-Bards of Cornwall. There is only one grade - that of Bard, robed in blue. But there are independent hereditary Druids of the blood in Cornwall too, feared by the established Order.

The Welsh Gorsedd of Druid-Bards. These are the famous Welsh Druids, horribly misnamed as there isn't a Druid in the entire official Welsh Order, as it is composed completely of Bards. But there are great and powerful Druids of Wales, feared by the established Order. The Welsh and Cornish people are demanding freedom in their Druidry as more Free Groves of Druids continue to spring up across those proud Celtic lands. In Wales there are always dark murmurings continuing against H.R.H. Queen Elizabeth IL Head of the Church of England, being the royal patron of the Welsh Eisteddfod.
Contact the Goredd via The Welsh national Eisteddfod Office. Cardiff. Wales.

The College of Druidism. The famous Scottish Druid Caledon Naddair, 4A Minto Street, Edinburgh EH9 I RG, Scotland, runs this. Specialises in Picto-Celtic Druidry. Druid Ian MacArt of the Isle of Man and Argyll is reviving the National Order of Druids in Scotland . You may contact him c/o The Order of Druids in Ireland.

Druidry in Australia and New Zealand

The United Ancient Order of Druids (U.A.O.D.), as described above, reigns supreme 'Down Under' with 76.000 registered members between Australia and New Zealand. Here are some of their lodges with membership numbers in brackets of some of the New Zealand Druid Lodges, which will give you a good idea of their strength:

United Ancient Order of Druids in Australia

Druids House, 302 Pitt Street, Sydney, New South Wales, Australia. Lodge, 407/409 Swanston Street, Melbourne, Victoria, Australia Lodge, 220 Currie Street, Adelaide, South Australia.
Lodge, 4 Roseberry Avenue, South Perth, Western Australia. Druids House, 71 John Street, Launceston, Tasmania, Australia. United Ancient Order of

Druids in New Zealand

Druids Chambers, Lambton Quay, Wellington, New Zealand - over 6.250 members! Grand Lodge of Canterbury, Druids Buildings, 227 Manchester Street, Christchurch, New Zealand - 2, 311 Members!

Otago and Southland, Druids House, 108 St. Andrew Street, Dunedin, New Zealand - 1,632 Members!

The U.A.O.D. is also organised in the U.S.A. and in Europe, chiefly in Germany, Norway, Sweden, Denmark, Switzerland, Holland and France.

The official address of the Ecole Druidique de Gaules (E.D.G.), The French College of Druidry, is: 17 Rue Etex, Paris, France. Tel. Paris 01 42 26 24 82. You may also contact one of their Chief Druids, Druid Boer Lingon, Clairière de l'Asgarde, 9ier Rue de L'Ysior, 17340, Chatelaillon, France. Tel. 46 56 26 10. And as we leave France the best contact there is Dr. Michel Raoult, author of Les Druides - Les Societes Celtiques Contemporaines -The Druids, Contemporary Celtic Initiatory Society, 4th edition, Du Rocher (Paris;, not yet published in English translation. This book is brimful with information on hundreds of Druid Orders worldwide .

The Druid in the New World

Modern Druidry in the U.S.A.

In America there was little interest in the Druids outside of academic circles. While many people knew little about the Druids, they generally accepted that the Druids were the priests of the ancient Celts, and that was that. The new Druid revival in America began independently of any direct Irish, British or French influences.

Because America (like Ireland) was spared the eighteenth century English-based Druidic revivalism, it was not bound by the traditions of those revivalists. In fact American Druidry did not start out as a religious movement or even as a Celtic appreciation society. Of all things, it started as a humorous religious protest. In 1963 a group of students at Carleton College in Northfield, Minnesota, rebelled against the college's mandatory chapel attendance requirement. For their protest they formed what they called the Reformed Druids of North America (RDNA) and held pseudo religious ceremonies once a week. Initially none of these students were pagans or heathens, or whatever insulting epithet Druids are usually called by: most were Christians, a few Jewish, and their services or ceremonies took on the forms with which they were familiar. Because Carleton College has a large Asian studies department there was a considerable amount of Eastern philosophy mixed in with their freethinking style (importantly, they would not have known that free-thinking has always been an important element of Druidry).

Their protest had the desired result and in 1964 the mandatory chapel requirement was repealed. Much to the surprise of the college authorities, however, the RDNA, enjoying their 'new religion', continued to hold services and meet once a week.

In time the new RDNA adopted most of the external practices now common among neo-Druidic groups: the eight festivals, a simple elected hierarchy and almost no dogma. The new group sought inspiration primarily from Asian and Middle Eastern living traditions.

Robert Larson was one of the original members who was one of the first to observe a seriously Celtic emphasis which years later would set the foundation for what has become known as the neo Druidic outlook. As the first 'Druids' graduated in Sixties U.S.A. from Carleton and moved out into the world they planted a new grove of RDNA wherever they settled. down. At one point there were about a dozen RDNA Groves across seven states, most fading by the end of the Seventies and the Hippy era. It is noteworthy that the Berkeley Grove, led by Robert Larson, was among these offshoots. From this Celtic oriented Grove the American neo-Druidic movement found its first avatar, Isaac Bonewits. Thirty years ago in 1974 the RDNA promoted to the post of Archdruid a man who had the distinction of possessing the only accredited degree in magic from the University of California, the late great Philip Emmons Isaac Bonewits saw great potential in the neo-Druidic movement.

He decided that the RDNA, or the new RDNA that he formed in 1975, was not the proper vehicle to promote Druidry. Bonewits decided that among the RDNA's faults was its refusal to call itself exclusively neo-pagan

(This Irish Archdruid would disagree as I refuse to accept the derogatory term 'pagan' for so illustrious and intellectual a movement as Druidry, but I digress). Back in the Seventies, however, the RDNA found that, like most self-styled neo-pagan movements, it had a phenomenal lack of effective organisation beyond Grove level.

In 1978 Bonewits carried some elements of the RDNA with him and founded a new neo-Druidic group that became known as Ar nDraiocht Fein, the Irish for Our Own Druidry, and, simultaneously, the initials. A.D.F. stood for A Druid Fellowship. The new A.D.F. had a slow start, but worked its way up to being the largest neo-Druidic group in North America.
It shared the top spot with the American Druid Order, The Henge of Keltria. The Henge surged ahead due to Bonewits resignation from the ADF on New Year's Day 1996. He stated his intention to function solely as a writer on neo-Druidry and he was highly successful. A.D.F's strength admittedly lies in its insistence on academic excellence in all scholarly research into Celtic and Druidic subjects. One of their mottos is: "Why not Excellence?" Another is: "Fast as a speeding oak", which points out that these things take time. A.D.F., existing in a multicultural society, makes no claims to an unbroken lineage or bloodlines of Celtic or Druidic descent. A case in point is that they do not require their members to be of Celtic descent or any such lineage., unlike Irish, British and most European druid orders. According to the A.D.F. it is possible for a Druid to be Amerindian or Afro-American or Asian American.

Former members of A.D.F. have broken off to form variations of the American neo Druidic revival.
Examples of these new branches of the Tree of Druidry in the 'new world' include The Henge of Keltria led by Tony Taylor, who have been interested enough in purist Irish Druidry to contact our Order of Druids in Ireland.

‒
U.S. Druid Tadhg McCrossan formed Uxello Druidicatos based on the French Gaulish traditions of the ancient Celts. Janette Copeland's Divine Circle of the Sacred Grove is something of a paradox - while it identifies itself as a Druid Order, its emphasis is split between Wicca and Amerindian:. spirituality (OBOD in England is going through similar schizophrenia).

The Primitive Celtic Church, founded by 'Gwyddion', has its emphasis on the French Gaulish traditions at their most basic and primal level. Then there is the American Druidic Church founded by Jay Tribbles MD.

A few branches formed independently of both RDNA and ADF. The first is The Druidic Craft of the Wise, which later changed its name to American Druidic Wisecraft. A Druid called Barney Taylor, who is also known as Father Eli, formed it. His form of Druidry seems to be a mixture of every conceivable esoteric philosophy thrown together. Who is to argue with that? Another branch is called Druidic Teaching.

Yet another branch of American neo-Druidry is found in The New Forest Center, founded by Douglas Momoe. Its emphasis is based on the Welsh Celtic tradition centred around the Arthurian legends and Merlin in particular. This puts Druidry into a specific context as can be seen in Douglas Momoe's book The 21 Lessons of Merlin, of which the Chief of an English Order, Philip Carr-GolDt-n of OBOD, says he cannot approve - but I could certainly approve of it in preference to the wacky new Wiccan Druidry of OBOD

Most of the other American branches of Druidry are a form of nature worship, which calls on Celtic archetypes, or gods or goddesses as focal points, some of it very creative and highly inspirational.

Unfortunately some American Druidry is at a point where there is considerable Wiccan influence, but this is only to be expected in a transitional period when Wiccan priests and priestesses in the States are changing over to become Chiefs of Druid Orders, as happened in England some fifteen years ago. It seems, as in Ireland, that some Wiccans are not content in their covens anymore.

This is due to the fact that they think they are also Druids, or they are genuinely 'caught' between both traditions..In time, as in England and Ireland, they will choose one path or the other under guidance. Currently there are far more books about Wicca in North America than there are about Druidry. But this is rapidly changing as the Wiccan books are left on the shelves and the Druid books swiftly snatched up. That said, modem Druidry owes a lot to Wicca for "setting the scene". Otherwise they are palpably different traditions. American Druids, and indeed the Druids of Ireland, Britain and Europe, are increasingly coming together and deciding what is and what is not Druidic. Wiccan elements are being distinguished from traditional Druidic teaching and practice and separated out. But, try as you may, you can't mix Wiccans and Druids. This is not to mean that we have to be enemies. It simply means that we oscillate at different frequencies and should not be allowed in the same room! Historically too, we could not be further apart. America, nourishing Druidry for barely forty years, will discover this for itself. As it does, it is fortunate in having Druids of the Olde Worlde standing by to help and guide.

U.S. Druid Archives

You can write or access over the Internet the famous Carleton College Druid Archives, International Druid Archives (I.D.A.), Carleton College Archives, 300 N, College Street, Northfield, Minnesota 55057, U.S.A. The most exhaustive Druid Archives in the world are in the New York Public Library.

North American Druid Orders

New Reformed Druids of North America (founded by Robert Larson and Isaac Bonewits). Contact P.O. Box 6775, San Jose, California 95150. Among its Groves and Affiliates the main ones are:

Schismatic Druids of North America And
Hassidic Druids of North America
Also
Orthodox Druids of North America (Irish based Druidry) Robert Larson. Contact: Grundy, 820 Circle Court, South San Francisco, California 94080

Divine Circle of the Sacred Grove, founded in 1981. Contact 1710 W. Camelback Rd., Phoenix, Arizona 85015, U.S.A. Founded by the famous Janette Copeland.

Ar nDraiocht Fein - A Druid Fellowship (A.D.F.), founded by Isaac Bonewits. Contact P.O. Box 516, East Syracuse, New York 13057 - 0516. This is Irish!

A.D.F. is also at P.O. Box 9420, Newark, DE 19714 - 9420, U.S.A.

American Druidic Church. Derived in 1985 from the Divine Circle. Contact 19060 Cajon Boulevard, San Bernardino, California 92407, U.S.A. (Jay Tribbles).The Henge of Keltria. Founded in 1988. Based on the Irish mythos. Contact P.O. Box 48369, Minneapolis, Minnesuta 55448, U$.A. Tony Taylor/

The Primitive Celtic Church, Founded in 1992. Contact P.O. Box 28646, Seattle, Washington State 98118, U.S.A. Founded by Gwyddion, a veteran of the A.D.F.

The Druidic Society. Primarily Bardic. P.O. Box 278, Kent, Ohio 44240, U.S.A.

Society of Reformed Druids. P.O. Box 389019, Cincinnati, Ohio 45238, U.S.A.

The Druidic Teachings. 3106 Crescent Avenue, #27 Marina, California 93933. Founded by Daniel Hansen, Druid, Doctor of Metaphysics and author of American Druidism: A Guide to American Druid groups, 1995

The Celtic Studies Center. This centre is devoted to education in the Celtic tradition. It guides its students in the direction of Druid societies most suitable to their development. Contact 27013 Pacific Highways South, #315 Kent, Washington 98032.

The Ancient and Royal Order of Druids, c/o David DePaul, Mog Ruith, Hollow Hill Grove, Aquarian Cooperation Network, 2205 Luella Street, Kalamazoo, Mi 49001, U.S.A. The Grand Lodge of Ireland founded this (Molesworth St., Dublin 2).

MetroDruidz Nus Grove, P.O. Box 3495, Jersey City, New Jersey 07303, U.S.A.

Druuidica Comardiia Eriutalamonos. Contact Michel-Gérald Boutet, 582 Bvrd des Prairies, Laval, Quebec H7V 1B5, Canada, qui, depuis la disparition de Tom Cross c'est rattaché à la Comardiia Druidiacta Aremorica Uecorectus citee plus haut

The Bard's Circle c/o Chaplain, P.O. Box 6531, Station 'A', Toronto, Ontario M5W IX4, Canada.

American Druidic People and Projects

Computer Druids c/o Erynn Rowan Laurie, Seattle. Email inisglas@ seanet.

com Frank McEwen Owen The Sacred Grove Centre/The Nemeton Project, 2301 Pearl Street, Box 74, Boulder, Colorado, 80302. Email theoakseer aol.com.

Mara Freeman M.A., P.O. Box 3839, Carmel, CA. 93921 Email chalice<mredshift.com. Finally, you can procure the most comprehensive documentation on all matters of Celtic interest from The Celtic League American Branch (CLAB),
P.O. Box 20153, Dag Hammarskjold Postal Center, New York, NY 10017.

MY NEXT BOOK

THE CELTIC ORDER OF MYSTERIES

Yeats sought a compromise within himself between his aims for a distinctive Irish culture and his magical interests. He tried to create a Celtic Order of Mysteries. From 1895 on he had a dream of making Castle Rock in Lough Key, County Roscommon "an Irish Eleusis or Samothrace".
Through mystical notes he wanted to initiate young men and women in this worship. He succeeded in enlisting Maud Gonne's sympathy for this idea of a castle of heroes and was deeply involved with it in 1897 and 1898.

He spent two weeks in April 1898 with the MacGregor Matherses in Paris, devising rituals for the Order, and he involved his uncle George Pollexfen. William Sharp. Mary Briggs, Annie Horniman among others in the work.

Various drafts of rituals and accounts of explorations and divinations are contained in material now in the National Library of Ireland. I had permission to examine and copy them there, in writing, by hand. They may not be photocopied for fear of damage to the paper by heat. It is all the more difficult to copy them there at a desk as Yeats had the most dreadful almost indecipherable handwriting. But his plans for this Celtic Order of Mysteries did not entice Maud Gonne out of her nationalistic politics and the idea was eventually abandoned.

I write this because I think this is what some here are more interested in than any Druid Order. Yeats. a senior Golden Dawn Adept had a good idea...

I was invited to give before the Dublin Theosophical Society at their fabulous old world headquarters and library at 31 Pembroke Road, Dublin 4. I was honoured to stand at the exact same podium from which Yeats had addressed the Society in the very same room with the library to the rear, on a fabulous Sunday evening. It would have been an ideal Society for me except I gathered that Blavatsky could not be questioned. The Secretary wrote out a cheque to me afterwards over tea and buns to cover my expenses.

I left with an elderly gentleman and walked down the broad quiet leafy avenue that had housed the upper middle class denizens of Anglo-Irish Dublin in another, more genteel age. As we walked he spoke of an ancient Druidic Queen of the Britons and made out her name to be Bua Dica, from two words - one from an ancient language similar to Gaelic he maintained, Bua meaning "Victory" - and Dica from the Latin meaning "I Declare". making her name to have been BuaDica, "Victory, I Declare" !

> "Beyond the Triple Spiral
> On the fair side of the Sun
> A dragon roars in a cave
> Under a world that's just begun."

Epilogue

LOVE BEFORE TIME BEGAN

by Michael McGrath

In his great temple of Newgrange the Archdruid of Ireland smiled contentedly as he watched his druids prepare for the winter solstice. The crystal window in the roofbox was being polished by the lovely druidess Lana, she was to be wed that very night. Not long to go now, he mused, until Prince Karnak, from the land Canalis out in the western ocean, arrives for their magical initiation in the sacred chamber.

An elder came up to the archdruid and reminded him: "Archdruid, it's almost time for you to light the ritual fire at Tara. The high king awaits you there."

"Ah, my good brother druid, the young king is always fretting about the psychic fires of Ireland. Have we not tended these sacred energies for aeons without fail? Alright, summon my chariot, the eyeless Mogruith will speed me through the firmament like lightning."

He turned to Lana; "Leave the crystal window and ready yourself to be wed to your prince."

The archdruid placed his hands on her shoulders as he towered over her. She thought a rather serious look had appeared on his long, haggard face. "Is anything amiss, my lord Archdruid?"

"Not at all, child, a thought just struck me..."

"What, my lord?"

"Lana, you are a bright young druidess. Look after your prince well, for one day people will search in vain for his great Land of Canalis...
A tall figure in a wine-black robe crystallised in the doorway, he hovered in silence.

"There, the Eyeless One who can see all around with his whole head, arrives to dispatch me to Tara. I shall arrive there instantly , for he is the most magical of druids." Lana bowed her head in respect in the direction of the shimmering Eyeless One.

 "Yes, my lord Archdruid, for he is the one who lives through all the millennia." In a flash they were gone.

Lana and her prince were wed at midnight. She felt so deliriously happy lying there alongside him in the sacred chamber of Newgrange. All night long they made love. Just as they reached the greatest ecstasy of all, blissfully united as one, the most fabulous light began whirling through the crystal skylight, split into many colours spiralling all around them, glowing coloured criss-crossing shapes in crosses, rings, diamonds, waves and curves...

Prince Karnak leaped to his feet in awe...but relaxed as he heard the melodious voice of his beloved Lana;

 "Sit awhile, my love, and lie with me here a little longer within this holy womb of the world. It happens on this morning every year, called the Nameless Day , it is the vital force, I know I am now with child, our divine child."

Deliriously they made love again, the light went and, exhausted, they slept for a time. Lana awoke to see Mogruith hovering over them, Karnak lay asleep.

"Do not awaken your prince, Lana."

"Mogruith, I am with child as foretold."

"Yes, your child will be the first of a whole new generation here, for your prince's land lies this terrible morning at the bottom of the western ocean. We were out there and could do nothing as it went down in flames."

"Shall I tell Karnak?"

"Not yet, fair druidess, he will learn it from his own god Lugh, for Lugh survives as his forces of light won."

"I feel so sorry for my poor prince with his land no more."

"Do not be so, Lana, for he shall go and build a great temple in the land of Isis in the East, while in the west the great ocean will bear your name forever."

'Ait-Lan-Tis' , Mogruith intoned, "the land of great power..."
Lana looked down upon her sleeping love as Karnak stirred. When she looked up the Eyeless One was gone.

*****

Midsummer Day was being celebrated on the Hill of Tara with hundreds of people there. A TV crew, some press photographers with Nikons, Canons and Hasselblads, huge lenses and tripods go about their work recording all the rituals and pageantry. Their journalist colleagues happily interview anybody who will talk to them in their quest of bringing the news of the return of the Irish druids to the world.

Scores of druids and druidesses , hands joined and raised, participate in the ancient ritual of the crystal on the royal mound of Tara.

The chant from the circle is like the hum of hundreds of honeybees. Suddenly a pure white light emits from the crystal atop the Lia Fail Stone of Destiny and spirals up into the clear blue sky.

A young couple sit and watch the magical energy working of the modern druids from atop the nearby Mound of the Hostages.

"It's just like old times, so wonderful again", Lana sighed wistfully.

"Yes my love, it's a pity Mogruith is not here with us to enjoy it", replied

Prince Karnak.

"Ah but you will never learn, my prince, see - he is here!"

"Where?"

"See the long silver haired one in the golden spectacles, dressed in that old wine-black robe whose colours keep changing - see it is he, Mogruith, in the midst of yonder gathering upon the Mound of Cormac", pointed Lana.

"Yes, indeed it is he, it's amazing for all he told you has come to pass, shall we hop over and greet him?"
Just then Mogruith turned in their direction and nodded.

"No, Karnak, he knows we are here, there's no need now, he has many earthly affairs to conduct here this day."

They slide down the grassy mound and wave in the direction of Cormac's mound.

Mogruith, the eternal druid, waves back.

ODI = The Order of Druids in Ireland

About the Author

Aged 76, Michael McGrath has been an active Irish druid for the past 30n years since he led the Return of the Irish Druids to Tara at Midsummer 1993.

He is a professional photographer since he trained under the late great professional, Oliver of Kilkenny, High Street studios, in 1966. He worked for the Munster Express, Waterford, The Kilkenny Journal and the Kilkenny Standard as a photo journalist and columnist. He started as an Executive Officer in the Dept of Local Government, Custom House, Dublin in 1964. His hobbies are reading, gardening, socialising and conversation. He has been researching and writing this book for a quarter of a century - his motto in life is "Festina Lente" - hasten slowly! He lives in a townhouse in Kilkenny city. He was educated at the CBS Kilkenny, Waterford Institute of Technology and Trinity College Dublin (degree in computer science).

www.ingramcontent.com/pod-product-compliance
Lightning Source LLC
Chambersburg PA
CBHW071341080526
44587CB00017B/2920